The Fooditor 99

Where to eat
and what to eat there
in Chicago

2020 edition

Text and photos by
Michael Gebert
for Fooditor.com

for my three tablemates, S., M., and L.

ISBN:

D1280093

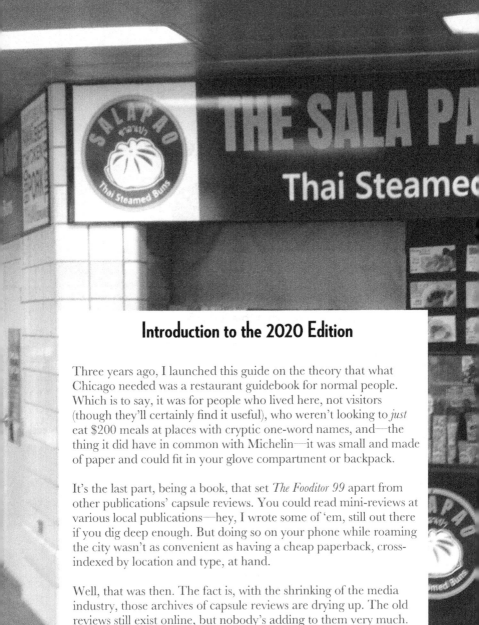

Introduction to the 2020 Edition

Three years ago, I launched this guide on the theory that what Chicago needed was a restaurant guidebook for normal people. Which is to say, it was for people who lived here, not visitors (though they'll certainly find it useful), who weren't looking to *just* eat $200 meals at places with cryptic one-word names, and—the thing it did have in common with Michelin—it was small and made of paper and could fit in your glove compartment or backpack.

It's the last part, being a book, that set *The Fooditor 99* apart from other publications' capsule reviews. You could read mini-reviews at various local publications—hey, I wrote some of 'em, still out there if you dig deep enough. But doing so on your phone while roaming the city wasn't as convenient as having a cheap paperback, cross-indexed by location and type, at hand.

Well, that was then. The fact is, with the shrinking of the media industry, those archives of capsule reviews are drying up. The old reviews still exist online, but nobody's adding to them very much. Which means that there's a distinct chance that a pretty good restaurant in a less-than-white-hot neighborhood, a restaurant in the honorable second tier, won't get written about by *anybody*, ever. Same for the traditional restaurant, Thai or Mexican or whatever, that isn't the *one* of its kind that everyone is talking about this year.

To me, that's just a shame. This is a fascinating city for food, so much more than the couple of neighborhoods that get most of the attention. If we're just directing visitors—and *ourselves*—to those few hot areas, we're missing so much, and selling ourselves short to the world. No wonder media can ping-pong so quickly from "Chicago, best dining city in America" to "Chicago is so *over*."

So this book exists to help you get out of those ruts. It goes all over the city, to find the cool things that are happening here. Picking 99 sounds definitive, though I wouldn't say it's meant to be the "99" best—that would be a familiar and somewhat static list. Instead, it's more like the 99 things I'm excited to tell you about, right now. To do that, I've cut a number of favorites from previous editions, not because they're not still good—it's more like they've graduated. When I see Mexican or Chinese or soul food places I've helped champion turning up on other publications' lists, it's time to find the next ones. Given a choice between the place you already know and the one you don't yet, this book is all about setting out to explore what's new—and maybe, in the process, finding love.

Michael Gebert
November 2019

NEW *indicates a new listing;* REVISED *a significantly rewritten review.*
F *points to a past story on the restaurant at Fooditor.*

1. Schwa

Wicker Park • Fine Dining, Tasting Menu • $$$$
1466 N. Ashland, Chicago • 773.252.1466 • schwarestaurant.com

Our first course came—described, deadpan, as their version of an Arnold Palmer cocktail. The joke was that at first glance, their version was about as far from *anything* in that sentence, especially a cocktail, as you could get. A large square of grass on a wood frame, plopped on the table in front of each of us, with a shotglass and a golf ball on a tee… and otherwise, it was various powders and herbs and spoons of goo, and the idea was to mix them in the shotglass, two or three at a time, and shoot back… the dry ingredients.

Alinea did something like this once—a grid of flavors, for you to eat with lamb. Their version was coolly scientific, dinner for Spock. Schwa's, on the other hand, just made us laugh—dinner of the absurd, from Monty Python or maybe Ernie Kovacs.

Owner-chef Michael Carlson's restaurant has been arguably the most influential place on our dining scene of the last 15 years, convincing us that brainy, funny fine dining could come from storefronts in farflung neighborhoods, without the formalities of waiters or fancy stemware and with the cooks in view and whatever music they felt like blaring overhead. But not taking yourself too seriously means others may fail to as well, and I can hear readers (not you, of course) thinking—*Schwa, it's fun, it's crazy, but the best restaurant in Chicago? Really?*

Really! Under chef de cuisine Norman Fenton, the rock and roll restaurant sharpened its game without losing its playful spirit, making food more beautiful than anything before it, geometric shapes decorated with edible flowers (at least, when it doesn't have a joke to tell). It was also more refined in terms of flavors— balancing citrus sharpness with lush and luxe ingredients and Asian influences that Schwa has rarely had before. The quintessential Schwa dish on this visit was a wagyu course—but instead of the near-cliché of a few slices of A5 beef, the dish was a bao (very well made) with the fatty-lush beef chopped inside, accompanied by radishes coated in butter. And so the fanciest ingredient of the night was introduced offhandedly as "your bread and butter course."

Fenton has left to work in Tulum since my summer '19 visit, but no place has been better than Schwa at home-growing talent, so whatever comes, I feel like it's in an accomplished place. That said, Schwa is still Schwa— dorm room dark, music turned up, BYO, and the kitchen will sometimes pour the wine they think you should have, not the wine you brought, and they will be appreciative of gifts, and you never know where that might lead…. The most important difference for some who suffered through closures for "plumbing problems" in the past is that it's now on Tock—so you *can* get a reservation, and it will actually happen. *What to order:* tasting menu. REVISED

F Meet the Chef Behind the Most Interesting Dish in Chicago, 8.21.18
Wilson Bauer On Running the More Grown-Up Schwa, 8.15.17

2. Jeong

Noble Square, West Town • Fine Dining, Tasting Menu, Korean • $$$
1460 W. Chicago Ave., Chicago • 312.877.5016 • jeongchicago.com

Hanbun, which Dave Park and Jennifer Tran opened
in an Asian food court in suburban Westmont, was a
delight, especially when it closed its counter window
and served a Korean-American tasting menu in the
kitchen. But it could have been taken as a bit of a stunt.
Jeong is the full-fledged restaurant that proves looks-
too-young-to-be-the-boss Park is a rising master, while
fiancée Tran, a gracious hostess, watches over the
room which, in Korean style, screens out the street
outside and welcomes you to its cozy inner sanctum.

There are two ways to go here, and unusually, they are
distinctly different. Even as the dishes often have
Korean names or shapes, the tasting menu—at $87,
eminently reasonable and not excessive—shows that
Park was paying attention in his French classes at
cooking school. There's classical poise and balance as
well as imagination in dishes like a ring mold of salmon
tartare studded with the crunchy pop of rice crackers,
or beautifully cooked bavette steak served with a
bearnaise-like "kimchi truffle emulsion," both the fungi
and the pickled cabbage just wisps of flavor on the
wind. I'd start with the tasting menu to get the lay of
the land, knowing that my reward would be Park's
desserts (he's his own pastry chef). Surprisingly, here
you'll find the strongest Korean influence of the night,

Dave Park at Jeong

earthy comfort-flavors like the caramelized doenjang on a financier or the ginger in a shortbread.

Then I would come back and order a la carte. The Korean flavors come through more strongly even in dishes as simple as a combination of broccoli and apples served with smoked mayo and chili oil. Pork mandoo (dumplings) seem classic to the form, while tteokbokki (seemingly the font of inspiration for Chicago's Korean-American chefs, between Passerotto and here) go wild with spicy mustard, chili sauce and a quail egg. There's a lot to discover here, and it's only the beginning for this couple. *What to order:* tasting menu; sashimi, yukhwe, tteokbokki, kalbi jjim, duck confit. NEW

F Hanbun's Intimate Korean Tasting Menu—in a Westmont Strip Mall, 7.28.16

3. Oriole

West Loop, Near West Side · Fine Dining, Tasting Menu · $$$$
661 W. Walnut, Chicago · 312.877.5339 · oriolechicago.com

I look forward to an annual return to Oriole more than any other high end restaurant—you can debate which you find the most culinary exciting (though if it's not in your top 3 or so, you have issues) but Oriole is, hands down, the most relaxing, transporting, the one that makes the world melt away as you enjoy the comforts of a special place—dining as spa day.

Chef Noah Sandoval's food makes masterful use of luxe ingredients, taking them in directions that are unexpected yet logical and balanced—there's usually something mixing delicate seafood flavors and Spanish *jamon* (Malpeque oyster, ham consomme and finger limes), pristine uni kissed with delicate flavors (as simple as yuzu and smoke), a simple pasta with shaved truffle, a foie course with fruit accents (huckleberry on a recent menu), a wagyu course, and even a bread course—nothing pedestrian about their long-proofed breads, spread with top quality butter. If the mere recitation of top level ingredients doesn't sound entrancing, that's the difference between a shopping list and the actual experience of dining here, each course a little bejeweled present (things are mostly small here, though you won't go hungry). And of the warmth of the service under the direction of Sandoval's wife Cara, whose first restaurant job this is. *What to order:* tasting menu. [REVISED]

F Dinner Among Friends at Oriole, 4.4.16

4. Kyōten

Logan Square • Japanese, Sushi • $$$$

2507 W. Armitage, Chicago • 312.678.0800 • kyotenchicago.com

Last year Otto Phan's eight-seat sushi bar Kyōten was a promising start just in terms of its format—high quality fish, served in the highly personal style of an eight-seat sushi-ya omakase (with a particularly jocular sushi chef). We didn't have one of those, of such quality. But on a return visit some months later, Phan is plainly doing more than merely *meeting* the expectations of his format and price point.

His sushi has the complexity and profundity of dishes in any tasting menu restaurant. This begins with his well-documented (including by Fooditor) eccentric preferences—for an oversize strain of sushi rice and a strong vinegar profile, that make nigiri feel like a slice of fish atop a mouthful of briny pebbles. But beyond that, each piece seems a fully composed dish, a subtle, deeply intuitive pairing of a fish, its texture and its temperature with whatever additional ingredient will not only highlight its nature but make it something new and memorable—otoro with a hint of smoke and citrus, octopus tossed with an avocado dressing, the fat, lobster-sweet Royal Red shrimp from Alabama, brushed minimally with a rich stock reduction made from its own shells.

Just as importantly, the flow of the meal is more refined than it was at the beginning, muscular cuts blended with delicate bowls of Asian flavors, so that it

has the pace, dare I say even the *plot,* of a fine dining meal, taking you on a tour of the sea's sensations. In the end, like any tasting menu, it's a chance to forget the world outside (or the plainness of the room itself) and disappear... for an hour or two... into one chef's magic. (P.S. F— Michelin.) *What to order:* tasting menu.
REVISED

F Otto Phan Is Here To Make Chicago Great Sushi, At Last, 9.13.18

5. Fat Rice

Logan Square · Chinese, Brunch, Bakery · $$$
2957 W. Diversey, Chicago · 773.661.9170 · eatfatrice.com

Fat Rice originally started with a repertoire of dishes taken from, or inspired by, the food of the Portuguese colony of Macau—mixing bright Asian heat with the deep funk of braises and charcuterie. But Macau is a small place with only so many native dishes. Now Fat Rice has jettisoned almost all of its original menu (save its eponymous *arroz gordo)* to expand into new territories, from Malacca to Goa, and to invent dishes built on that basic model of funky depth—from housemade sausage, from Spanish canned fish, from fish sauce and shrimp paste—paired with bright notes of spice, coconut milk sweetness, tamarind sourness and so on. This is "Chinese" food that you burrow into and let warm you from the inside out, fundamentally different from any other in America.

Besides the main restaurant, there's The Ladies Room, a dark bar straight out of a Marlene Dietrich movie, and The Bakery at Fat Rice, which offers drinks and pastries and cookies inventively reflecting Asian sweets, as well as some savory items that make it easy to squeeze into this busy place for a convenient bite. *What to order:* sardinhas furosos, favas guisados, bacalhau, chili prawns, lacasssa, rice crisp. REVISED

F See What You'll Be Eating at The Bakery at Fat Rice, 7.5.16
Fat Rice: Searching For the Authentic Macanese Cuisine, 3.7.16

6. Smyth & The Loyalist

West Loop • Fine Dining, Tasting Menu, Farm To Table • Smyth: $$$$ Loyalist: $$$
177 N. Ada, Chicago • 773.913.3773 • smythandtheloyalist.com

No restaurant in Chicago treats dinner as quite so much of a rabbit hole to go down as Smyth. Behind almost every dish there is some sort of process— fermentation or curing or something to alter its fundamental nature. Chefs John and Karen Shields, veterans of Charlie Trotter back in the day, work with a farm near Bourbonnais to grow interesting things just for them, yet the relentless tinkering with the form of foods makes it seem like actual foods aren't enough— they have a desire to invent new ones.

And sometimes they're pretty spectacular, like the signature dessert—an egg yolk cured in anise until it's as chewy as candy, served with a soft meringue and on top of a bit of jam. The most recent time I went, our server explained that the meringue was prepared in a Pacojet, an expensive device normally used for making gelato quickly. It wasn't taken all the way to freezing— just far enough that it would hold the right creamy texture for an hour or two. If you think about it, the dish is basically just egg yolk in a bed of egg white, but changed beyond immediate recognition into something marvelously, unmistakably *new* in your mouth.

And so dinner goes—if you recognize the main ingredient, you'll be puzzled by what's around it, koji for an alien-seeming Japanese fermented taste, farro for a bit of crunch. All this mystification of cuisine, rooted a bit in Noma, comes in a relaxed room, more a living room than a dining room, with the cooks working quietly and calmly behind you. Somewhere else there might be solemn art gallery pretension to how such creations are presented to you, but not here. *What to order:* tasting menu (various sizes available).

* * *

The Loyalist, the downstairs lounge and bar, tends to be a bit overlooked, at least by writers if not diners. What started as a more direct and straightforward use of the stuff their farm was growing has morphed into one of those bars doing decadent luxe foods, with caviar servings and truffle add-ons—the category of Roister and Au Cheval. And it's the most consistently successful and interesting of that bunch, taking its tone from its celebrated burger, with bacon ground into it and a marmite spread—but deliberately humble-looking and a little misshapen, something you might stumble onto in a roadside diner. If the ingredients are modest (cucumber salad) something like trout roe will dress them up; if the ingredients are posh (aged ribeye) the presentation (a puddle of black garlic goo) will tell you not to take them too seriously. The goal is rich, indulgent pleasure, and The Loyalist delivers on that. *What to order:* burger, deviled eggs, smoked whitefish Caesar, pork belly chop, ribeye. REVISED

F Chicago Restaurant, Kankakee Farm, 6.22.16

7. Elske

West Loop • Nordic, Tasting Menu • $$$

1350 W. Randolph, Chicago • 312.733.1314 • elskerestaurant.com

Elske gets more interesting every time I go there. David and Anna Posey's Nordic-inspired cuisine always makes me wonder how you can delight people with such austere ingredients, flavors that run the gamut from dark green to brown, so to speak, yet manage to seem luxurious even in bitterness, making a wintry landscape feel lush. Some, it's not that mysterious—the "risotto" made of celeriac and green apples has plenty of butter to make it lovable. And smoked trout's pleasures are simple but hard to miss, especially when accented by honey and beets. There's so much creativity going on in the interplay of seafood and vegetable flavors in these dishes that the ones built on roast meats, however satisfying, seem less engaging by comparison. Anybody can glaze a sweetbread, but pairing octopus with cucumber, ground cherries and spiced tofu... I'm not sure there's anywhere else on earth that that seems logical, yet it fits right in.

And after an evening of these woodsy intellectual challenges, Anna's grandma's-house-comforting desserts—equally made up of words you've never seen together before—make a warm conclusion to the meal. *What to order:* there's a tasting menu, which includes the now-famous foie tart dusted with parsley powder, but I find making my own menu of nearly everything on the seasonal a la carte menu the more attractive option.

F A Short Chat With Anna and David Posey of Elske, 12.9.16

8. Kumiko

West Loop, Near West Side · Cocktails, Tasting Menu, Japanese · $$$
630 W. Lake,, Chicago · 312.285.2912 · barkumiko.com

You know Kumiko is from the Oriole team from the moment you walk in—you pause in the entry way for a welcoming sip before being ushered into the restaurant, a soothing interregnum between the clamorous world and the comforts to come inside. The simple, wood-trimmed room hints at Japan without being a cartoon of it, and the same is true for the food and drinks—the concept is built around bartender Julia Momose, who grew up there.

So the cocktails are primarily shochu and sake-based, plus a few highballs reflecting the Japanese taste for whiskey; a short list of deconstructed cocktails, like a Sazerac accompanied by tastes of the ingredients going into it; and a list of food half the length of the cocktails. (Which for a party of four made it easy—we ordered everything.) That, at least, is the primary experience, though you can also score a bar seat to have Momose tailor cocktails to your exact tastes, or reserve a spot at Kikkō, the omakase sushi bar in the basement.

The question was, would we be full after eating the whole menu? We half-joked about finishing the night with burgers at The Loyalist, and after the first few bites, it looked like we might have to. Things were quite tasty—warm oysters with a buttery dollop of caviar, very nice tempura shrimp with a squiggle of mayo—but lusher than they were filling. Two main courses were also, in a way, deconstructed—loup de mer and short rib accompanied by a host of ways to flavor the protein, from furikake seasoning to a pork-fat-enhanced mayo. The latter was so good we ordered it twice—and surprisingly, by the end, we were full after all, ready for the small taste of Japanese milk bread with ice cream and shaved Perigord truffle that ended the meal. (When they tell you to order four of those for four people, believe them.)

Small, expensive and often wildly precious, not least in its assumption that a menu seven or eight items long is plenty to choose from (don't choose, just order it all), Bar Kumiko is a place that your steak and potatoes grandpa would mock throughout the entire experience. For me, like at Oriole, it was precisely calibrated magic, every item that seemed to be setting them up for mockery delivering on an almost giddy delight, from the cocktails with distinctive flavors ringing changes on familiar recipes to the lush, but not overindulgent, food. How often I could return is a question with a food menu this short, but the first time was an utter charmer. *What to order:* sashimi, tempura prawn, steam buns, gyudon, Japanese milk bread. **NEW**

9. Wherewithall

Avondale • Fine Dining, Tasting Menu • $$$

3472 N. Elston, Chicago • 773.692.2192 • wherewithallchi.com

Before dining at the new restaurant from Johnny Clark and Beverly Kim (Parachute), I felt I was asked a *lot* whether my party had allergies or dietary restrictions. Partway through I understood why: the menu only listed four courses, but we'd already had about five things, which were only described to us as they arrived. So our only chance to object was upfront.

And honestly, "I'll just sit down and you bring me food" is fine by me. It started with hummus and various farmers market vegetables fresh from the ground to dip in it, as well as little mini beignets and a dip like bacalao. Everything that followed was fresh and clean, bright and simple flavors, whether it was seared rare tuna served in a summery green sauce and with a single umami-rich dehydrated tomato, or a bowl of many-colored beans and a cured egg yolk that tasted like caramel, or the dessert, a semifreddo dotted with currants, mint leaves and almonds.

It's $65 for four (more like eight or nine) courses, in a sunny room with light fixtures with felt shades, like mushroom caps overhead. Surprisingly, unlike Parachute, there's no discernible Korean influence here (Kim is Korean and Clark has spent time there); here it's just bright, welcoming American food, and an utter delight. *What to order:* tasting menu, optional cheese plate; there are "wine snacks" in the bar. **NEW**

10. S.K.Y.

Pilsen • Fine Dining, Asian, Brunch • $$$
1239 W. 18th, Chicago • 312.846.1077 • skyrestaurantchicago.com

Foie bibimbap is exactly the sort of upgraded Asian food that could go so, so wrong. But take your first bite and it is… simply really good bibimbap; foie is what shoots it into the stratosphere. That experience is what you will have, more often than not, at S.K.Y., named for chef Stephen Gillanders' wife Seon Kyung Yuk. She also designed the restaurant, inexpensively but handsomely into a dark, atmospheric hideout at one end of the Pilsen strip, just west of Thalia Hall.

Gillanders' background was many restaurant openings around the world for Jean-Georges Vongerichten; he landed in Chicago, setting his price point more modestly—like the hamachi sashimi that subs swollen black sesame seeds for caviar's pop—but still demanding a high level of execution. (The chef's counter ought to come with the proviso that you'll be gazing right into an intense kitchen.) The payoff is dishes that mix Asian flavors and affordable luxury with unusual deftness; Charles Ford, a Bristol veteran, keeps the room relaxed and comfortable, while pastry chef Tatum Sinclair's desserts offer a sunny ending to the meal (and a cheerful presence at the chef's counter). *What to order:* hamachi sashimi, lobster dumplings, fried chicken with fermented hot sauce and creamed corn, foie gras bibimbap, sea bass.

F Nine Ways To Get To Know Pilsen's New S.K.Y., 11.30.17

11. Virtue

Hyde Park · Southern, Soul Food, Brunch · $$
1462 E. 53rd, Chicago · 773.947.8831 · virtuerestaurant.com

The danger with an upscale attempt at something like soul food is that you can lose the working class charms of joint food by fancying it up. Erick Williams spent a couple of decades working his way up to head chef in the decidedly upscale MK restaurant in River North, so the danger certainly seemed real. Yet almost everything I tried at Virtue hit the sweet spot of tasting like grandma made it, while showing off superior kitchen skills.

So there was beautifully cooked catfish, and delicate fried green tomatoes with shrimp remoulade, and a tender pork chop big enough to take a nap on, but also terrific greens with smoked turkey that were straight from grandma's pot, and damn near platonic ideal of banana pudding. The space—previously A10's in a vintage Hyde Park building—gives the area a rare touch of unaffected glamour, while Williams' commitment to nurturing his own neighborhood-based workforce (giving them the chance that Michael Kornick once gave him, walking in off the street) adds to the good vibes of a good place.

What to order: changes seasonally, but Southern classics like shrimp and grits or blackened catfish nearly always please, and the "small rations" portion of the menu makes good use of Southern-style pickling, as in the Butcher's Snack plate. **NEW**

Erick Williams at Virtue

12. Blackbird

Near West Side, West Loop • Fine Dining, Tasting Menu • $$$
619 W. Randolph, Chicago • 312.715.0708 • blackbirdrestaurant.com

Blackbird has been arguably the biggest trendsetter of the last 20 years in Chicago, sending cooks, a love of bold and often porky flavors, and the idea that restaurants should be minimalist, loud and lively all over town. Yet it's also been a changeling restaurant, reinventing itself with the chefs who have taken over as Paul Kahan oversees a growing empire. The current chef de cuisine, Ryan Pfeiffer, came up through David Posey's kitchen after some time in California, and there seems a bit of a Californian touch right now, with dishes that are very direct in their presentation of a few fresh flavors, usually plated all in the middle (so you have to taste everything together, he says).

The West Loop being what it has become, Blackbird under Pfeiffer has to reconcile the poshness that current diners expect with the restaurant's historically unpretentious outlook, and he offers a variety of levels to eat at (although your table isn't getting any further from the next one regardless). What you see across them is a commitment to careful treatment of local and ocean product that avoids overdressing plates—a kind of American brasserie approach that says (in Kahan's characteristically blunt fashion) buy good things, add one flavor to bring out what they are, and cook it perfectly—and if you don't screw up along the way, you're a great restaurant. *What to order:* changes more or less monthly; there are tasting menus at $85 and $185, and one of the best deals in town is the $28 three-course lunch. REVISED

F Trying To Keep Blackbird's Soul in a Michelin-Driven World, 10.25.19
Blackbird Is One Of The City's Top Kitchens. And Now, It's Ryan Pfeiffer's, 4.14.16

13. Monteverde

West Loop • Italian • $$$

1020 W. Madison, Chicago • 312.888.3041 • monteverdechicago.com

Chicago has a reputation as an Italian-American city, though when you try to tally up the standouts in Italian food, the list gets kind of short pretty quickly. One was always Tony Mantuano's high-end Spiaggia, especially under Sarah Grueneberg as executive chef. When Grueneberg opened her own place (with fellow Spiaggia alum Meg Sahs) in late 2015, she made it more accessible pricewise, all to the good, but more than that, she did it her way—for instance, liking the way that woks crisp up noodles in Asian cooking, she had them installed in her Italian kitchen.

The menu is partly divided into classics and her creations *(pasta tipica* and *pasta atipica)*. But really everything shows Grueneberg's mastery of Italian technique—cacio whey pepe and tortelloni di zucca are Platonic ideal versions of classic dishes—as well as the confidence with which she can bend Italian food into whatever she feels like. One must-have now is burrata e ham, which combines puffy little lard biscuits from Sicily called *tigelle* with burrata and country ham. Only Texas-born Grueneberg could make one of the best Italian bites and one of the best Southern bites in town out of the same dish… and that dish is a *ham sandwich. What to order:* burrata e ham, 'nduja arancini, cacio whey pepe, wok-fried arrabiata, ragu alla napoletana.

F Making Pasta to Order With Sarah Grueneberg at Monteverde, 1.11.16

14. Daisies

Logan Square • Italian, Farm to Table, Brunch • $$

2523 N. Milwaukee, Chicago • 773.661.1671 • daisieschicago.com

When it opened in mid-2017, Daisies was a very promising
neighborhood restaurant, a farm to table spot (chef Joe
Frillman's brother brings them produce from his farm in
the northern suburbs), making pasta in Italian styles without
being explicitly Italian—for instance, taking pasta in a
Nordic direction with the beet agnolotti with dill and
smoked trout roe. Since that time Daisies has only gotten
better—and I have found myself recommending it to people
regukarly, and more than almost any other place at its
eminently reasonable price point. The simple, supple
housemade pasta is delightful to eat, whether it's strands of
chitarra popping with the instant summer of sungold
tomatoes, or pappardelle in a hearty ragu. You literally
cannot go wrong eating pasta here, but that's not all that's
happening—they're busy curing and preserving things to
eat and drink. So especially outside of peak summer, both
the food and drink menus show off funkier flavors—you'll
find everything from the house raspberry soda with a
vinegary tang to beet and green bean flavors in cocktails.
What to order: pasta!, seasonal vegetable dishes, summer
tomatoes with bone marrow, onion dip.

F Seven Places That Led Joe Frillman to Daisies, 7.11.17

15. Proxi

West Loop • Cocktails, Asian • $$

565 W Randolph, Chicago • 312.466.1950 • proxichicago.com

Emanuel Nony's Sepia has long been the Armani suit of
downtown dining—well-tailored for any business function,

but executed by Chef Andrew Zimmerman with modern creativity that makes it a more sophisticated choice for the expense account crowd. Still, nothing about Sepia made you think that their followup was going to be a glamorous bar and lounge serving south and southeast Asian street food. Yet their bet on the growing sophistication of Chicago's taste for Asian flavors seems to be paying off, especially when the flavors are captured with such clean precision.

The showpiece is a wood fire grill, and it's easy to see why things like candied Indonesian Pork Jerky or BBQ lamb ribs go over well, but I was at least as impressed with things off the fryer—like the halibut collar, succulent fried fish to be picked apart and eaten with a funky Thai garlic-chili sauce —and by the vegetable-heavy first two thirds of the menu: sugar snaps served with a bruléed yuzu kosho miso, a citrusy bite of summer, or "black pepper pork," a bowl of crumbled pork and peanuts made to be rolled up in lettuce leaves for a brightly crunchy bite. *What to order:* elotes, crispy Vietnamese crepe, octopus with fava bean hummus, fried fish collar, coal roasted oysters, Indonesian pork jerky, black pepper pork.

F How Asian Street Food Came To a Downtown Hood at Proxi, 7.6.17
A Pastry Chef Does the Chicago Marathon, 10.4.17

16. Birrieria Zaragoza
Archer Heights · Mexican · $
4852 S. Pulaski, Chicago 773.523.3700 · birrieriazaragoza.com
There's an unconscious tendency to treat great family restaurants in a heritage tradition like Mexican food as accidental miracles—as one housewife's cooking might be,

by sheer luck, better than that that at the next house. Zaragoza is the epitome of the Mexican family restaurant—deep roasted goat flavors, handmade tortillas as comfy as your favorite blanket, and eyeopeningly bright salsas, served by two generations of a sweet family in an old Polish diner. But don't think that there aren't serious craft chops and thinking at work here—from carefully shopping for local goat to preparing it in a way descended from French consommé, the Zaragoza family are skilled and savvy cooks, and second-generation Jonathan has worked around town (Sepia, Masa Azul) and puts on occasional pop-up dinners with other cooks or to show off things besides his family's homey menu. In this tiny space, they carry on the traditions of Mexican cooking in America—and show what its future is. *What to order:* goat consommé with housemade salsa; quesadillas. REVISED

17. Elizabeth

Lincoln Square • Tasting Menu, Farm to Table • $$$
4835 N. Western, Chicago • elizabeth-restaurant.com

It's been a busy year for Iliana Regan—she closed Kitsune, launched and promptly sold out a glamping spot in Michigan, let Jenner Tomaska take over Elizabeth for the summer, published a memoir, and got longlisted for a National Book Award, the first food writer to do so since Julia Child. Some might wonder if Elizabeth, her original restaurant, was going to be a bit forgotten in all this, but I suspected that catching her in fall after a few months in the woods would find her at her most inspired, and I was not disappointed. A succession of vegetable-forward dishes were little magical tastes of the growing midwest—sungold tomatoes with farmer cheese in shoyu, al dente green beans diced into a tartare, with egg and toasted pistachios—accompanied on the non-alcoholic pairing by equally inventive things to drink, like a purple corn tea/cider, or a kind of yogurt drink with coffee, lemon and tarragon, good enough to be a savory dessert. The climax came with skate —admittedly *not* a midwestern fish—delicately breaded in cornmeal and served in a vegetable/mushroom sauce as green as a pond... exquisite minimalism.

As a space, even with an open kitchen Elizabeth is relaxed and cozy, a little less goth than it used to be (or maybe that's just Michelin plaques crowding out the deer skulls), but still a little bit of whimsical woodsy comfort in the city—a hobbit-hole, and that means comfort. *What to order:* with Elizabeth, you don't so much pick what to order as when to go, depending on which menu theme is up at a given time, prices of which vary considerably. Best thing to do is get on her mailing list and see what's coming up. REVISED

18. Galit

Lincoln Park • Middle Eastern • $$$
2429 N Lincoln, Chicago • 773.360.8755 • galitrestaurant.com

Hummus—hard to think of a more ubiquitous dish this side of French fries, and like a plate of fries, what's not to like, and what's to remember an hour later? But then there's Galit, where there's a whole section of the menu devoted to hummus whipped to a transcendent creaminess out of Rancho Gordo chickpeas—you can have it relatively simply with aleppo pepper, or with trumpet mushrooms and gribenes, or with mint and sumac and "way too much olive oil," or with brisket and braised carrots. (All of this comes with pita from the wood-burning oven, puffed like a balloon.) Whichever way you go, it's a testament to the goodness of simple dishes, and to Israeli cuisine (which chef Zach Engel learned both in the country and at restaurants like Shaya and Zahav) as a distinct thing with highlights—

falafel that tastes like spring in a crunchy little fried ball, labneh a bracing blast of creamy tartness, and so on.

That's one side of Galit, but more than just Israeli food, it's about Jewish cooking. So entrees are simpler and more comforting than starters, drawing more from hearty Eastern European cooking than the Levant—cabbage rolls with deeply caramelized tomato sauce on top, chicken thighs with harissa and peas in whipped feta, etc. (Which are things that admittedly can be heavy, and do not always have the instant likability of the middle eastern dishes.) Like many restaurants that take a bargain cuisine to a higher level, Galit's prices may induce a little menu shock, but the jam-packed dining room suggests that people get over it quickly for the sake of food with this warm a heart. *What to order:* first time, it makes sense to order "The Other Menu," a prix fixe with options by category; either way, be sure to get any of the hummuses, the salatim (basically a platter of noshes including ezme and labneh), fried fish, chicken thigh, stuffed cabbage. **NEW**

F Coffee With Zach Engel and Andrés Clavero of Galit, 2.12.19

19. Middle Brow Bungalow
Logan Square • Beer, Pizza, Bakery • $$
2640 W. Armitage, Chicago • 773.687.9076 • middlebrowbeer.com

A tribute to the many forms of magic yeast are capable of, Middle Brow started as a brewery working out of other facilities, and has progressed to this sunny rehabbed industrial building where the beer may well be outclassed by the baking of Jess Galli, who baked in various spots around San Francisco before moving back to Chicago. Lunch or dinner at Middle Brow Bungalow might start with a big hunk of brown bread, dense and malty, and some soft butter sprinkled with sea salt—elementally good and almost impossible not to devour completely, even if you know you have a pizza on the way. The pizzas take a similar dough, sourdough with a four-day retard, and top them with farmers market-fresh ingredients like squash with salsa verde—this is true *cuisine de Logan Square,* fresh and earnestly straightforward utilization of midwestern veggies (there's some meat toppings available, but pretty much as afterthoughts). In lieu of pizza, one of the salads, which lean toward sharp, peppery greens, would make an equally good and more balanced accompaniment to that wonderful bread. *What to order:* any bread, any pizza, any salad. **NEW**

20. mfk.

Lakeview • Seafood, Spanish, Wine Bar • $$
432 W. Diversey, Chicago • 773.857.2540 • mfkrestaurant.com

Step down into this small space and you'll feel like you've escaped to sunny Spain even when the snow is blowing outside. The menu, under its young chef Alisha Elenz, takes an admirably direct approach to simple, mostly seafood dishes, and the restaurant as a whole takes an equally direct one to modestly-priced, likable wines and welcoming service. That's all there is to say, except that I wish we had many more like it. *What to order:* boquerones, albondigas, fideos, smoked trout toast, basque cake.

F mfk. Has a New Chef. A Very New Chef, 2.13.18

21. Boka

Lincoln Park · Fine Dining · $$$

1729 N. Halsted, Chicago · 312.337.6070 · bokachicago.com

The Boka Group's original restaurant reinvented itself with the arrival of chef Lee Wolen, who'd once lived across the street but came to it by way of Eleven Madison Park in New York. Wolen basically set out to make arty tasting menu food in normal plate quantities, and that philosophy of delivering superior execution while taking a couple of steps back from preciousness pervades the entire restaurant, which has a clubby comfortableness (and a wall of quirky pictures embedded in moss in its patio room). *What to order:* Wolen made his name doing roast chicken, and it's fine in whatever form it takes now, but his Asian-tinged octopus dishes are always strong, and no table should be without a plate of the roasted carrots.

22. Munno Pizzeria & Bistro

Uptown · Italian, Pizza, Wine Bar · $$

4656 N. Clark, Chicago · 773.942.7575 · munnochicago.com

In a time of big concepts, Munno's motto seems to be "let's get small." The space is a cafe wrapping around the corner of a building, looking out on a park. The staff is welcoming and unpretentious. The short menu has half a dozen pizzas, half a dozen pastas, and a couple of salads, all made in the tiny kitchen (the bar of the cafe it used to be, now crammed with cooking equipment). What makes this place a little masterpiece of modest ambitions is that everything is beautifully made, whether classical Italian dishes like lasagna that's only a half inch or so thick and layered with ragu and béchamel sauce, or Neapolitan-style pizzas (even though the oven is not woodburning) with a supple crust and a few simple toppings. It's the definition of a neighborhood charmer, with a sign of true commitment to its in-house diners in its strict no-take-out, no-delivery policy. *What to order:* salumi plate, ravioli, lasagna bolognese, eggplant parmagiana, any of the pizzas.

F The Best Restaurant of 2018 You've Never Heard Of, 10.24.18

23. Entente

River North • Fine Dining, Tasting Menu • $$$
700 N. Sedgwick, Chicago • 312.285.2247 • ententechicago.com

Having moved from Lakeview to River North, Entente is as close to being a new restaurant as a place with the same owner, chef and name can get—a tasting menu spot of delicate little bejeweled dishes ingenuously accented with playful flavors, reflecting chef Brian Fisher's heritage at Schwa (but jettisoning the rap music and general funkiness it had in Lakeview). So, a little less distinctive as an experience than the original, rougher-edged Entente, but at its best—usually involving lush seafood—Fisher's plates can be transcendently lovely. There is a downside, though, in that—like Schwa, like Alinea—Fisher relies on sweet flavors, candied little cubes and sauces, which pop on any single dish, but wear on the palate over a dozen courses, if you do the tasting menu. I was worried where a meal like this could go for dessert, but pastry chef Jared Bacheller (Boston's L'Espalier) offers comparatively savory desserts that restore balance. *What to order:* tasting menu; hamachi kama, berkshire pork belly, Long Island duck, anything seafood. REVISED

F Is Lakeview Ready For an Entente With Fine Dining?, 10.17.16

24. The Bristol

Bucktown • Italian, Farm to Table, Brunch • $$$

2152 N. Damen, Chicago • 773.862.5555 • thebristolchicago.com

The combination of pork and pasta love, beer and cocktail connoisseurship, and a willingness to go there with offal meats and other oddities, all in a casual setting, made The Bristol under Chris Pandel one of the most influential restaurants of the last decade in this city. (We can't *entirely* blame it for the communal tables fad.) Now under Todd Stein, The Bristol still shows off bold, direct cooking, not always Italian in flavors by any means, but Italian in its philosophy of working in a straightforward way with the flavors and products of the midwest. At the moment, the monthly three-course menu built around one ingredient (such as corn or tomatoes) is an outrageously good deal for $29. *What to order:* autumn salad, cacio e pepe, duck egg raviolo, Amish half chicken, skirt steak, anything that looks good. REVISED

25. El Che Steakhouse & Bar

West Loop, Near West Side • Steak, South American • $$$

845 W. Washington, Chicago • 312.265.1130 • elchebarchicago.com

El Che Bar has reconcepted to stress the new "steakhouse" in its name, but honestly it's hardly any different, which is the good news—it remains a good choice for a group that wants meat, but not *just* meat. The darkly chic room is dominated by the Argentine grill at the far end, an inferno chef-owner John Manion and his crew tend like guys shoveling coal in a steamship. Everything here comes from it—no fryers, no induction burners. But they find more subtlety in using it than you'd expect, rounding out the meats—the parrilada includes steak, short rib, morcilla (blood sausage), marrow bone and more—with fresh vegetables (hard to find in South America) and lighter things like grilled quail and swordfish, as well as the empanadas that Manion's other restaurant, La Sirena Clandestina, is known for. *What to order:* Parrillada, BBQ quail, Parisian gnocchi, creamed corn, heirloom tomatoes and melon. REVISED

26. Honey 1 BBQ

Grand Boulevard • Barbecue • $
746 E. 43rd, Chicago • 773.285.9455

After struggling in Bucktown for several years, Honey 1 pitmaster Robert Adams moved to the south side, and he's never seemed happier than now with an appreciative crowd for his generously meaty cuts of Chicago barbecue, slow-cooked for maximum smoky flavor in an "aquarium" glass and steel pit. *What to order:* Rib tips, hot links, brisket. Take-out only.

F Touring Chicago BBQ With Texas Monthly's Barbecue Editor, 12.11.15

27. Osteria Langhe

Logan Square • Italian • $$
2824 W. Armitage, Chicago • 773.661.1582 • osterialanghe.com

There's too little regionality in Italian food in Chicago—or maybe it's dominated by the brusque flavors of one region, Sicily—so a neighborhood restaurant devoted to the Langhe and Piemonte is to be cheered on that basis alone. The food of chef Cameron Grant makes skillful, satisfying use of the region's meats and cheeses (it's as Swiss-leaning as it's stereotypically Italian), not to mention its white Alba truffles in season, while owner Aldo Zaninotto, a wine importer, covers that end with well-chosen recommendations. The result is a restaurant that just gets better and better at finding honest pleasures in the food of one region —a model for what Italian food ought to be now. *What to order:* vitello tonnato, plin, tajarin, coniglio.

28. Table, Donkey and Stick

Logan Square • Wine Bar, European • $$$
2728 W. Armitage, Chicago • 773.486.8525 • tabledonkeystick.com

I was long a fan of this Alpine-inspired restaurant starting under chef Scott Manley, who set its pattern of housemade charcuterie and lots of cheese on the first side, and some simple but completely satisfying roasted fish or meat dishes on the flip side. And there was everything to like about the reasonably priced wine chosen by owner Matt Sussman, who also started the in-house bread program that brought a crusty rye baguette to your table. Under the latest chef, Justin Moser, there's *still* everything to like, from the crusty baguettes and the housemade charcuterie to the simple, but perfectly well-made entrees. Sussman's goal was to evoke the kinds of intimate places you might find in the Alps, and though he can't do anything about Armitage Ave. being flat as a board, this is exactly the dark and cozy hole to crawl into for a good meal and equally good wine. *What to order:* schweinekopf, duck liver mousse, grilled carrots, pan-roasted whitefish, Berkshire porkchop; wine fans should watch for the Tuesday night wine nights, where interesting producers' bottles are poured more or less at cost.

Berthe Montes Garcia at Xocome Antojeria

29. Xoco

River North • Mexican, Sandwiches, Breakfast • $$
449 N. Clark, Chicago • 312.723.2131 • www.rickbayless.com/restaurants/xoco

I've always thought Xoco ought to put up a sign saying "Same Great Airport Taste!" No one else would want to, but Rick Bayless' Tortas Frontera stands at O'Hare are widely considered about the tastiest airport eating in America, built on produce from the same farmers as his other restaurants. And honestly, River North has a certain resemblance to an airport (crowds, taxis, fast food and Starbucks everywhere, bros talking loudly on phones). So it makes sense that Xoco, Bayless' sandwich shop on the corner of the block where Frontera Grill and Topolobampo are, overlaps with the airport sandwich menus, while adding some less portable potables like soup. If you have to be in that area for lunch and want to spend lunch prices, it's an obvious, happy choice. *What to order:* breakfast, chorizo-egg torta, chilaquiles, smoky bacon mollete; lunch, Baja chicken torta, torta ahogada, Cubana, tortilla soup. **NEW**

F The Farmer, The Airport Sandwich, and the Future of Food, 12.14.18

30. Bar Biscay

West Town, Noble Square • Wine Bar, Spanish • $$$
1450 W. Chicago, Chicago • 312.455.8900 • barbiscay.com

Saturday afternoon, a friend and I are sitting at the bar at Bar Biscay, drinking vermouth and noshing on a plate of little fishy pintxos, on sticks or slices of bread, maybe fresh or maybe out of cans... simple, grownup (kids would never touch these fish), relaxed and unpretentious. This for me is the essence of Spanish food, not something you can reduce to a set of flavors ready to be reproduced by a chain of restaurants, just the promise that every day has the chance to wind down and give itself over to a glass and funky flavors straight from the land and sea. Larger than the same group's mfk., and definitely flashier with its lighting meant to evoke glitzy coastal discos in the 70s and 80s *(voulez-vous couchez...)*, Bar Biscay offers a range of experiences, now from executive chef Alisha Elenz, who also runs the same group's similarly Spanish, simple and wonderful mfk. *What to order:* on the dinner menu, salted hake brandade, fideos, razor clams, loup de mer; pintxos, whatever looks good.

31. Pretty Cool Ice Cream

Logan Square • Ice Cream • $
2353 N. California, Chicago • 773.697.4140 • prettycoolicecream.com

Dana Salls Cree is a veteran of chichi places from Alinea to Noma to Blackbird, but in the end she wanted to make ice cream that everybody could afford. The result is this utterly charming ice cream bar shop, easily the happiest thing to open in Chicago in ages, from the colorful multilevel seating space (ideal for kids who like to climb) to the window that lets you see ice cream bars being made. The flavors range from rich-tasting custard and buttermilk-based bars to "plant pops" (using things like almond milk) and "truck pops" (dairy free and water based) with flavors like litchi lemon tea (from Rare Tea Cellars, naturally). Prices are a little higher than your local 7-11, given the quality of ingredients, but with little kid "pony pops" for just $2, she's putting the populist in artisan popsicles. *What to order:* mint cocoa nib chip, peanut butter potato chip, orange party pop, dark chocolate plant pop... there's no bad choice here.

F Life and Ice Cream Advice From Pretty Cool's Dana Salls Cree, 8.29.18

32. Xocome Antojeria

Archer Heights • Mexican • $
5200 S. Archer, Chicago • 773.498.6679 • xocome-antojeria.business.site

A Mexican mom and her son, who's worked in kitchens like Boka, run this little counter service Mexican spot on the southwest side, emphasizing tacos, tlacoyos (disks of masa stuffed with beans and topped with meat, cheese and veggies), breakfast tacos and other items. And throughout the menu, you see signs of their extra care with everything —offering blue corn masa as a tlacoyo option and piling them with carnitas that would make the reputation of a carnitas stand, working garlic and marjoram into the tamale masa, making their own tamarindo from scratch without sugaring the tart drink up. It's a gem worth the long haul (for most of the city) to the vicinity of Midway. *What to order:* tlacoyos, filet mignon taco or quesadilla, pambazo.

F Downtown Chef Works With South Side Mom at Xocome Antojeria, 11.29.18

33. Passerotto

Andersonville • Korean, Italian • $$$
5420 N. Clark, Chicago • 708.607.2102 • passerottochicago.com

The best explanation of Jennifer Kim's notion of Korean-Italian fusion is one of her dishes: gnocchi with a sensually meaty lamb neck ragu—except they're not gnocchi, they're ddukbokki, the springy rice cakes that are like boiled packing peanuts (this is a good thing). Not every dish here has as clear Italian-ness in its flavors and Korean-ness in its textures, but the idea of a common heritage of comfort, of maternal love in food form, comes through in most of her dishes, even as Asian spice and vinegar cut through to remind you that 'Rotto, we're not in Genoa anymore. What could have been a cracked concept instead proves to be a personal vision of a better cross-cultural world that you want to be part of. *What to order:* Ddukbokki, hwe dup bap, Sun Wah spiedina, short rib with Mama kimchi. [REVISED]

F Will Jennifer Kim's Passerotto Be "Korean Enough"?, 4.25.18

34. Bar Sótano
River North • Cocktails, Mexican • $$$
443 N. Clark, Chicago • 312.391.5857 • rickbayless.com/restaurants/bar-sotano

Rick Bayless may have a chef's empire in airports and grocery store products, but at the same time, unlike many name brand chefs, he's mostly kept his main restaurants confined to a tight area in one city where he can check up on them daily. And also to where he and his family are in their lives—so Bayless' first real bar comes along as daughter Lanie reached the age and (more to the point) the experience to help devise a list of cocktails. (If you doubt they're that hands-on, the first time I went was in a slush-storm, and as I walked in she was mopping up the entry way, while Dad was at the bar mixing cocktails.)

The cocktails aim for different expressions of Mexican flavors—tropical fruit focused, herbal freshness, spices, or conceptual (tasting like guacamole or al pastor tacos). The latter were a bit much for me, but the other three were very successful at capturing a Mexican sensibility, a more modern take on the easy-to-like tropicality found in tiki bars. (Ironically, Three Dots and a Dash is next door, making this the only block in town where the best drinking is consistently subterranean.) I would say the food is less complex than at other Bayless restaurants, befitting a menu aiming more for bar snacks than full entrees, but that doesn't mean it doesn't display the same virtues of farm-to-table ingredients and thoughtful use of Mexican flavors. Add in the relaxedly hip room, that looks like somebody's loft, and we're lucky to be drinking and eating in the same city where Rick Bayless keeps his restaurants. *What to order:* Oaxacan Drinking Snacks, tacos arabes, plancha-charred broccoli, Mexican paella. **NEW**

35. Band of Bohemia

Ravenswood, Lincoln Square • Fine Dining, Brunch, Beer • $$$
4710 N. Ravenswood, Chicago • 773.271.4710 • bandofbohemia.com

Band of Bohemia is the antidote to many things that you may be tired of in other high end restaurants—it's big (so you can often just walk in), located in a relaxed northside neighborhood, and focused on the beer with food and spice flavors that they brew in house. New chef Soo Ahn is a veteran of Grace and EL Ideas, and given that pedigree, his food's a little more artfully precious than it has been here before. Once or twice dishes seemed to have an extra element or two they didn't need—lamb saddle, on a gorgeous taleggio puree, would have done fine without a sweet-and-sour-sauce-ish ring around the plate.

But there was a beautiful "pineapple three ways" halibut dish that got more variations out of a one-note fruit than you would have guessed, deeply-flavored Parisian gnocchis with morels, and what will likely become his signature dish, a salt-cured carrot that turns a supermarket vegetable into a meaty main course (and made me think of Bugs Bunny eating a carrot with steak knife and fork). Bonus points, too, for the very smart move of making the $20 beer pairing free on Tuesday and Wednesday. *What to order:* seasonal tasting menu, or whatever looks good a la carte; beer pairing. [REVISED]

F Band of Bohemia Is Different, 3.14.18

36. Tempesta Market

West Town, Noble Square • Italian, Sandwiche • $$
1372 W. Grand, Chicago • 312.929.2551 • tempestamarket.com

Most days at Tempesta there's a huge, orange-red blob of meat on the counter, inviting you to come up and have a piece of bread schmeared with it. This is the 'nduja from owner Tony Fiasche's 'Nduja Artisans, a spreadable Calabrian pâté that's like butter crossed with hot salami, and it's on one of the sandwiches as well as mixed into one of the flavors of gelato—no, really. (That one's... *interesting.*) Anyway, business started with the 'nduja and now they make a bunch of other meats, for their own use and for clients nationwide.

And so their sandwich shop is more than a sub place—it's there to demonstrate what can be done with their meats (and others they carry) on crusty Publican Quality Bread, creating sandwiches that are really more like composed dishes than subs. They range from the Dante, named for the 'nduja's heat, to the Southside Johnny, which combines porchetta, cheese, broccolini and rosemary broth for dipping, and they're nearly always impressive for the care with which they're conceived and executed. And although it's decidedly a meat-oriented place, there are always salads, a soup or two, and one veggie sandwich—plus gelati that do *not* contain 'nduja. *What to order:* Dante, Southside Johnny, B. Franklin, meat and cheese board.

F Tempesta Market: Such Meats As Dreams Are Made On, 12.14.17

37. Pizzeria Bebu

Near North Side · Pizza · $$
1521 N. Fremont, Chicago · 312.280.6000 · bebu.pizza

Declaring something the best pizza in Chicago—you might as well stick your face into a fan. So much of it depends on what style you want at the given moment—deep dish, thin, Neapolitan, etc.—and especially when a pizza could be described as New York/New Haven style… look, you're gonna eat more than one pizza in your life, there's no *one* best pizza.

But I could make a case for Pizzeria Bebu, a small pizzeria hidden in the apartment buildings behind the chain-food-riddled New City complex at North & Clybourn. Bebu has a unique story—it grew out of the pizzas that pizzaiolo Jeff Lutzow would crank out for staff meal at The Publican, which gave him a chance to refine his crust (he uses a 48-hour retard) and play around with toppings (like taking a Publican side dish, ramps with romesco, and putting it on pizza). So what you get at Pizzeria Bebu is basically a very well made tossed and crispy crust, topped with something worthy of being a composed dish at a restaurant. If you're used to knocking back pepperoni or cheese without thinking about it, this isn't that kind of pizza—even a simple margherita has a bold, complex flavor of tangy cheese and brassy tomato sauce, and they only go up in assertive flavors from there. Besides pizza, there are some fresh salads and simple Italian-ish appetizers. *What to order:* margherita, little neck clam, puttanesca, taleggio… whatever looks good.

F They Turned Family Meal Into a Pizzeria of Their Own, 5.26.17

38. Tortello

Bucktown · Italian · $$
1746 W. Division, Chicago · tortellopasta.com

There's no better advertisement for fresh pasta than someone making it in the window at Tortello, cracking sunset-golden eggs into a mound of flour (read the Fooditor story mentioned below to find out how they get so golden-colored). What eventually comes from those eggs and that flour after much rolling and stretching is beautifully supple tortelli filled with burrata, chiusoni, bucatini and other pasta shapes. From there, you have two choices—buy the fresh pasta and cook it at home, or order off the menu, which is very well optimized for the best sauce/ingredients for each shape (the ingredients prepared by longtime Chicago chef Duncan Biddulph, who spent time in Italy as well as at Lula Cafe and Rootstock). Bright and noisy, the interior area is not exactly a romantic Italian getaway, though it gains in charm from the infectious presence of co-owner (with his wife) Dario Monni, an Italian who grew up around shops like this, then worked restaurants around the world before deciding Wicker Park needed a place like this. *What to order:* tortelli filled with burrata, chiusoni with saffron and sausage, lumache with beef ragu. **NEW**

F Making Pasta in a Window on Division Street, 7.24.19

39. Politan Row

West Loop, Near West Side · Indian, Middle Eastern, Vegetarian · $$
111 N. Aberdeen, Chicago · 312.278.3040 · chicago.politanrow.com

Revival Food Hall got the food hall model right, gather the best things around town in one place downtown, but they also pretty much nabbed all the best candidates, and most of what followed in their wake was pretty dire. Politan Row

is the first one since to find a way to make it work a different way, with a combination of startups out of the pop up/ weekend market worlds, plus a few new concepts from established restaurateurs. The result (ironically right next to McDonald's new HQ) is a collection of interesting, accessible places worth making the trek downtown or out to the West Loop for.

My favorite spots are two right inside the door. Start with LaShuk Street Food, a vendor of middle eastern food who's been at the Wicker Park Farmer's Market, for wonderfully fresh falafel and hummus. Next is Thattu, Keralan (regional Indian) food from Margaret Pak, who started cooking Keralite food at a pop up while she worked at Kimski; although a few dishes have chicken, this is perhaps my favorite stop in town to eat vegetarian, with dishes like the black chickpea curry or kimchi-based upma, most served with a choice of coconut milk rice or appam (a thin rice crepe). Don't miss the calicut, a kind of savory cookie full of deep Indian spice flavors.

Other offerings include Mom's, which does Japanese-Hawaiian comfort food, Bumbu Roux, which similarly mashes up Cajun and Indonesian rijstaffel dishes (Chris Reed did the pop up The Rice Table), Loud Mouth for high end hot dogs and other comfort foods, a branch of Floriole and more. If any budding Ray Kroc next door wants to create the *next* new American church, this would be a pretty good place to start looking for it. **NEW**

Margaret Pak at Thattu in Politan Row

40. Big Jones

Andersonville · Southern, Brunch · $$
5347 N. Clark, Chicago · 773.275.5725 · bigjoneschicago.com

Southern comfort food is common enough in Chicago, and
you could just take Big Jones on that level and enjoy it for
fried chicken and grits. But chef-owner Paul Fehribach is a
serious student of southern cooking—he already has one
cookbook devoted to recipes mostly derived from historical
cookbooks—and the more you dig into the corners and by-
ways of the menu, the more you're likely to have an
interesting and unusual experience. Even at brunch you'll
find dishes made with heritage grains, like the waffles made
with Carolina Gold rice flour, while lunch and dinner
feature dishes which aim to evoke an entire time and place
—chicken and dumplings are dated specifically to a
farmhouse in 1920, and I'm sure he has a good reason for
that. A renovation in 2018 modernized both the dining
room and the kitchen, and the cooking in general seems to
have take a step up since then, some of it attributable to
new equipment (the fried chicken is now pressure-cooked,
like the Colonel's, though the resemblance mostly ends
there) and some of it perhaps just increased confidence of
what they're capable of. *What to order:* boucherie board,
pimiento cheese with benne crackers, boudin balls, crispy
catfish, fried chicken, shrimp and grits, crawfish pie.

F Cooking With Heritage and Perennial Grains at Big Jones, 11.22.17

41. Funkenhausen

Ukrainian Village, West Town · German, Southern, Brunch · $$$
1709 W. Chicago Ave., Chicago · 312.929.4727 · funkenhausen.com

Funkenhausen is literally the name for a smokehouse in

Germany, but it's got a *farvergnügen-y* tongue-in-cheek sound that suits this playfully porky beer hall from Mark Steuer (Carriage House). He mixmasters his dual heritage—Germany and the Carolinas—into dishes like sturgeon pastrami topped with kraut and fish skin chicharron, ricotta dumplings with bits of kielbasa, or a wood-grilled ribeye with sauerbraten and "horsey" sauces. With every dish seeming to hit comfort notes and tangy and acidic ones at the same time, Steuer reveals himself to be a mad German scientist of Southern cooking, while it's hard not to have a good time in the big, deconstructed-beer hall room with a few goofily Disneyesque touches. *What to order:* pretzel, sturgeon pastrami, Sürfentürfen, charred broccolini, ricotta dumplings, 'Nawlins style boudin. **NEW**

42. Kimski

Bridgeport • Korean, Eastern European, Beer • $$
960 W. 31st, Chicago • 773.823.7336 • kimskichicago.com

The family behind Bridgeport's beloved Maria's bar is Polish-Korean, while chef and street artist Won Kim is Korean—so they came together over a shared love for pork and fermented cabbage to create this modernist beer hall combining craft brews (including their own Marz beers; they have a taproom not far away) with hearty Ko-Po fare. It's the kind of unpretentious cross-cultural good time with a beer and an egg on it that you can only have in Chicago. *What to order:* Maria's standard (Korean-polish sausage), scallion potato pancakes, pork belly bowl, Bing Bong Bowl, Ko-Po Beef, Kimski poutine.

43. Mako

West Loop, Near West Side · Sushi, Japanese · $$$$
731 W. Lake, Chicago · 312.988.0687 · makochicago.com

B.K. Park, known for Arami and then Juno, set out to bring
Chicago its first high end sushi omakase—and by the time
he finally got Mako open, he was the fourth in a sudden top
tier sushi boom. But no category of food is a zero-sum
game, and Mako deserves more notice than it initially got as
a worthy contender in its genre.

The room—the most handsomely appointed among the
new sushi spots—offers both seating at the sushi corner and
a small number of tables, depending on whether you want
to gaze at your chef or your date. Park's omakase divides
fairly evenly between nigiri, raw plates and cooked dishes,
which makes for a smooth-running meal that gives you a
pleasing variety of Japanese tastes over filling up on raw
fish. The nigiri is cut fairly small, meant to easily be one
bite; with at most one well-chosen topping, whether it's
fatty Ora king salmon with subtle pickled garlic, the clean
ocean taste of horse mackerel with ginger root and chive, or
wagyu with pepper soy—a Japanese idea of steak au poivre.
Among the cooked dishes, chawanmushi made with
umami-rich mushroom broth comes with crab meat buried
deep in its pillowy custard, while duck arrives in a bowl as
both breast and sausage slices in a ramen-like broth.

Another strength is the excellent beverage list, well-chosen
for both sake and wine. There's no need to pit the new
sushi stars against each other to pick a winner; Mako stands
on its own as a chef's full expression of the ideals he's been
working toward for many years. *What to order:* omakase. **NEW**

F Seven Things B.K. Park Wants To Make You at Mako, 5.17.19

44. La Mom Kitchen

Bridgeport • Chinese • $$
3312 S. Halsted, Chicago • 773.565.4431 • lamomkitchen.com

When La Mom Kitchen is good, it is very very good. Hong sue pork, a version of the lacquered pork belly dish also known by Chairman Mao's name, is platonic ideal level; that and a bowl of white rice offers more satisfaction than any two dishes elsewhere. La Mom's dumplings aren't officially xiao long bao, but they're better soup dumplings than any xiao long bao in town. From these I could see why other food writers had praised it so highly… which is why the other things I had on my first visit were so frustrating. Chicken broth with beautiful shaved noodles badly needed salt, at least for American tastes, and Guilin-style noodles in a spicy beef broth were ruined by the chilis being basically incinerated in the wok. Perhaps sudden popularity has caused sloppiness in the kitchen; in any case, it's a reminder that even with guidance from writers (like me!), it may take more than one visit, and a few false starts, to find your way to the best things a cuisine from halfway around the world has to offer. I'm pretty sure it's worth it… but I'm still getting there myself. *What to order:* La Mom's dumplings, hong sue pork, yang chow fried rice, jin cheng pork ribs, tang cu sweet and sour ribs, house fish filet noodles, cucumber in minced garlic, spicy cabbage stir fry. **NEW**

45. Cellar Door Provisions

Avondale, Logan Square • Bakery, Coffee, Farm To Table • $$
3025 W. Diversey, Chicago • 773.697.8337 • cellardoorprovisions.com

Cellar Door Provisions' mahogany-colored croissants are about the best in town and the dark, crusty bread is as bitter as coffee grounds; those Tartine cookbooks on the shelf have been put to good use, and as long as you're keeping none-too-early Logan Square breakfast hours, coffee and a pastry here is pretty terrific. Lunch is very natural, a little virtuous and definitely on the expensive side. Dinner started as an affordable prix fixe—not too much food, mostly veggie, relaxed and fresh-tasting and a bit of a relief next to epic tasting menus—an excellent date night. It's a la carte only now, but no reason you can't find the same virtues in the earnest, straightforward stuff they get from farmers and make for themselves. *What to order:* croissants, tartine, quiche; dinner changes seasonally. [REVISED]

46. Lula Cafe

Logan Square • Farm to Table, Breakfast, Brunch • $$
2537 N. Kedzie, Chicago • 773.489.9554 • lulacafe.com

Pioneering restaurant in both Logan Square and in doing farm to table cooking (when that didn't even exist as a term for it), Jason Hammel's Lula Cafe still has its hippie cafe charms—it's a little cramped in a creaky old building, and the art on the wall is guaranteed to be a bit weird. But the quality of the cooking has risen steadily over the years, and current chef-de-cuisine Andrew Holladay does a skillful job with Lula's menu of mostly comfortable entrees like roast chicken and pastas, presented in a way that highlights the clean-tasting appeal of top quality ingredients. *What to order:* changes seasonally; vegetarian tasting menu, Monday night farm dinner.

47. Aroy Thai

Ravenswood, Lincoln Square • Thai • $
4654 N. Damen, Chicago • 773.275.8360 • aroythairestaurant.com

Tiny Ravenswood Thai restaurant with a translated "secret" menu pointing to some of the more authentic dishes on the menu; the beef ball and tendon soup, eye-openingly spicy and pungent with tamarind and galangal, is one of my standard orders when I have a cold and I need a miracle cure. *What to order:* pad see eiw, basil pork with century egg, crispy salty fish fried rice, tod mun (fried fish cakes), beef ball and tendon soup.

48. 5 Loaves Eatery

Greater Grand Crossing • Breakfast, Soul Food, Chicken • $
405 E. 75th, Chicago • 773.891.2889 • 5loaveschicago.com

Sweet and welcoming African-American family-run restaurant, serving some of the best fried chicken—I mean, top 3—in town, and other comfort foods like shrimp and grits. But the real comfort here is the bond they form with their customers, who are liable to get up to give them a hug at any moment. *What to order:* fried chicken, po' boy sandwich, shrimp and grits (weekends only), salmon croquettes, lemon poppyseed pancakes, anything that comes with a biscuit.

F Meet the Nicest Restaurant in Chicago (And the Family Behind It), 10.21.16

49. Income Tax

Edgewater • Wine Bar, French, Spanish • $$$
5959 N. Broadway, Chicago • 773.897.9165 • incometaxbar.com

Named for both a vintage cocktail and the sort of low-scale business that blends right into a neighborhood, this wine bar with accomplished bistro food was embraced by its community for its easygoing, very welcoming ways—like the policy of letting you buy half an unopened bottle on its list, with the other half being offered by the glass to anybody in the place. Chef Ellison Park, a veteran of

Parachute, expanded the menu's flavors to take in the middle east (as in a great stewed eggplant with mint and charred cucumber) as well as the wine-producing regions of Europe. I really like the way the menu, which used to be pretty clearly divided between countries, now blurs their borders in deep, richly satisfying flavors. *What to order:* seasonal menu changes regularly, but there's something to like at any time of year.

F They Just Want To Be Your Neighborhood Wine Bar, Edgewater, 10.25.16

50. HaiSous Vietnamese Kitchen/Cà Phê Dá

Pilsen • Vietnamese, Sandwiches, Coffee • $$
1800 S. Carpenter, Chicago • 312.702.1303 • haisous.com

Thai Dang was a cook in Michelin-starred Ria, then he had an upscale downtown place (Embeya) with bits of Asian flavors. That imploded due to a partner's chicanery, and he and wife Danielle Dang put their two pennies (*hai sous* in Vietnamese-French) together and opened a mid-priced Vietnamese restaurant, HaiSous, with a daytime cafe next door.

And now I'm going to come out against the conventional wisdom. The setup implicitly makes you think that HaiSous is the main attraction and Cà Phê Dá the side gig. And yes, if you want dinner, HaiSous is a chic night out in an up and coming neighborhood (with occasional anti-gentrification protesters) that gives you bright, healthy-tasting Vietnamese flavors, executed with high-end precision. It's the kind of thing you come to the big city to have.

But Cà Phê Dá... first, it's like a movie set of a Vietnamese cafe, never mind that you have people in winter coats outside instead of street vendors and buzzing scooters. But the spell it casts continues with dishes like the exquisitely simple com gà, chicken flavor soaked deeply into rice, and the Vietnamese coffee drinks—especially the astonishing cà phê trúng, Dang's invention, coffee with a sabayon-like egg custard on top. It's one of my favorite hidden spaces in Chicago, a magical getaway and a delight to show off. *What to order:* HaiSous: papaya salad, grilled ribeye, roasted duck stuffed with kaffir lime leaves, whole fish, rice noodles with tofu. Cà Phê Dá: chicken or grilled pork banh mi, com gà (chicken rice), gỏi gà (chicken salad), cà phê trúng.

F Behind the Scenes With Refined Vietnamese Flavors at HaiSous, 7.14.16

51. Gaijin

West Loop · Japanese, Ice Cream · $$
950 W. Lake, Chicago · gaijinchicago.com

It seemed inevitable that Paul Virant (Vie, in Western Springs) would come back to the city from the suburbs, indeed to the West Loop where he'd been private events chef at Blackbird, back in the neighborhood's earliest foodie days. What no one expected was that he'd do it in a narrow Japanese-style bar specializing in okonomiyaki (savory pancakes, basically) and kakigōri, shaved ice desserts, a tiny, Osaka-cool place that's a rebuke to the sprawling bro taco bar catecorned to it and other such *obvious* offerings in the area. It exists partly because his wife spent time in Japan, but the real explanation, one suspects, is the Japanese affinity for simple, direct cooking—Virant compares okonomiyaki to pizza for the way you can make them with any ingredient you like, but it's obvious that as a okonomiyakiolo, he believes in the power of tradition and tried-and-true classics. *What to order:* go for the shrimp okonomiyaki first; house pickles, kakigōri. **NEW**

F Paul Virant is Coming Back to the Big City, 2.21.19

52. Bellemore

West Loop, Near West Side · Fine Dining · $$$$
564 W. Randolph, Chicago · 312.667.0104 · bellemorechicago.com

Bellemore chef Jimmy Papadopolous came to Boka Group through Lee Wolen, chef of the namesake Boka, and you'll recognize a similar approach, light and bright seafood dishes and salads and deeply comforting roasted meats and pastas. (Then there's Papadopolous's showpiece, the custard pie topped with an oyster, tiny flowers and an ounce of caviar; even at $69 for a tiny slice, the thing flies out of the kitchen and straight onto Instagram.) He seems undaunted by the scale of the showcase they've given him, a very cosmopolitan downtown spot big enough for aircraft, the interior designed by Karen Herold, who revamped her own Embeya, designed just a few years before in the same space. It's a big stage for a meal that's meant to impress, and at his best, Papadopolous has beautifully controlled flavors and highly attractive luxe dishes (he must have one of the biggest budgets for little flowers in town). *What to order:* venison tartare, sweet potato tots, grilled Spanish red prawn, grilled lamb belly.

53. Mozzarella Store

Near North Side · Pizza, Italian · $$
822 N. Michigan, Chicago · 312.285.2449 · mozzarellastores.com

This aspiring chain—note the plural in all the social media IDs—makes excellent fior de latte and burrata in house. This would only go as far as what you had to put them on, but thankfully the crust of the pizza is Neapolitan-perfect, crispy-bubbly outside and spongy inside. A margherita pizza was as good of its type to be had, with acidic tomato and their cheese; a more elaborate one, with ham, corn and mushrooms, should have followed Coco Chanel's rule and taken one thing off, so take that as guidance that simpler is better here. Beyond pizza, a salad with burrata, marinated eggplant and pumpkin seeds (I think) was a nice showcase for the burrata, too. There are also appetizers, paninis, a coffee and gelato bar with some breakfast pastries (my friend Kenny Z found them too refrigerated for their own good, alas) and a small deli section where you can pick up the housemade mozzarella, ricotta and a few other things to make at home. But the main news is that it brings Neapolitan pizza of this quality to the north end of the Magnificent Mile. *What to order:* pizza and salad—so far. **NEW**

54. The Albert
Near North Side, Streeterville • Fine Dining • $$$
228 E. Ontario, Chicago • 312.471.3883 • thealbertchicago.com

Larry Feldmeier worked for Thomas Lents and Nick Dostal at Sixteen when it was one of the last hotel restaurants still aiming for international acclaim and tire company glory. Now he's at a funky, Einstein-themed boutique hotel in Streeterville, doing food that comes closer to satisfying the routine wants of tourists—but giving it twists that lift it above most of what's along Michigan Avenue. The showpiece is the crispy chicken leg, orange chicken-y flavors taken back home to Chinatown by serving the entire leg, uncensored, all the way to chicken foot and toes. Not everything aims to shock quite like that, but it does aim to offer high quality craftsmanship with superior ingredients, artfully plated and with forward flavors that lift this place to a class above most hotel dining. *What to order:* heirloom tomato and plum stracciatella, crispy chicken leg, roasted stone bass, luna piena. **NEW**

F The Chicken Leg of Streeterville, or: Meet Chef Larry Feldmeier of The Albert, 8.7.19

55. Sticky Rice Northern Thai Cuisine

North Center • Thai • $$

4018 N, Western, Chicago • 773.588.0133 • stickyricethai.com

Sticky Rice appeared just as we were starting to learn that there was a difference between Bangkok Thai food and that from Chiang Mai and the north. (We may have initially been distracted by the presence of insect-based dishes on its menu, though.) For that reason I find its lengthy menu harder to pick through for gems than many, but at its best Sticky Rice embodies the contradictory joys of Thai food—bright heat and deep funk, a sense of profundity in cooking worth the effort. *What to order:* nam prik ong, northern Thai sausage, gang hung lay, pad num prik pou.

56. Cebu

Wicker Park • Filipino, Brunch • $$

2211 W. North, Chicago • 773.799.8650 • cebuchicago.com

After Bayan Ko, Cebu might be the next Filipino breakout restaurant, doing Filipino flavors with unusual care and subtlety—something like fine dining execution, well beyond what you expect from the casual atmosphere and thoroughly reasonable pricing. Adobo chicken was some of the best roasted chicken of any sort I've had lately; pork belly lechon was similarly deeply flavored, with gorgeous crackling skin, while Bam-I (pancit noodles) were first-rate, studded with slices of Chinese sausage. I recommend this family-run place wholeheartedly, with a couple of caveats to note: there's not a lot that isn't pork on the menu, so be aware of that. And the space—the former Birchwood Kitchen/Americano 2211—still has the small tables of its coffeeshop predecessors. The combination of big platters of food and eating the whole meal off tiny appetizer plates does this impressive food a disservice, but it's worth the struggle. *What to order:* lumpia, chicken adobo, Bam-I, Cebu lechon belly, garlic rice. **NEW**

57. Nha Hang Viet Nam

Uptown • Vietnamese • $
1032 W. Argyle, Chicago • 773.878.8895

Most non-Vietnamese visiting Argyle Street don't look much beyond pho, but for a fuller range of Vietnamese cuisine visit this family run spot with pretty minimal English but a James Brown-level vocabulary of spicy funk. *What to order:* rare beef salad, woven rice cake with pork, clay pot pork and catfish, bun mam, spicy crabs, mi quang, chao vit with duck.

58. Mi Tocaya Antojeria

Logan Square • Mexican • $$
2800 W. Logan Blvd., Chicago • 872.315.3947 • mitocaya.com

Peasant food with panache—that about sums up Diana Davila's Mexican food, which often starts with recipes from her family's heritage (which included a Mexican restaurant in Oak Forest). Like the dish labeled peanut butter y lengua, which was inspired by an uncle's dish of braised tongue in peanut sauce. But if humble in origin, the results on the plate burst with hyperrealist colors like a Mexican mural, the eye-opening spices equaled by the fluorescent splatters around the plate. *What to order:* peanut butter y lengua, queso fundido, enchiladas potosinos, fish con mole amarillo.

59. Flat & Point

Logan Square • Barbecue • $$$
3524 W. Fullerton, Chicago • 773.904.7152 • flatandpoint.com

The name refers to the parts of a brisket, the place has wooden benches and a giant drum smoker visible behind the counter... so it's hardly surprising that many come in expecting another Smoque. Instead, chef-owner Brian Bruns (Spiaggia, Tru) is here to take brisket and other smoked meats, cooked pure Texas style, in new directions. So an order of brisket comes not with fries and sauce, but plain and with a neat lineup of Hallenbeck potato slices and stewed kale. (It's also wagyu, for extra eyes-rolling-back richness.) The lead-in to your main course could range from housemade pâté to a smoked mushroom duxelle (a phrase that has surely never appeared on a menu in the Hill Country) or, for that matter, a pasta special. Does barbecue *need* to get fancy like this? Hey, Smoque is still there six days a week if you want a classic plate of 'cue. I'm more excited at this point to see someone master the art of smoked meat and then use it as one element in a composed dish—indeed, to take it places it's never been before. Bruns is still figuring out where that is, but it's intriguing to see him try. *What to order:* assume brisket and something from the charcuterie section to start, and go from there. NEW

60. Szechwan JMC

Chinatown • Chinese • $$
243 W. Cermak, Chicago • 312.929.2212 • szechwanjmc.com

You'd better like the tingly, aluminum foil mouthfeel of Sichuan peppercorn if you try this Sichuan restaurant—because you're going to get a lot of it. Sometimes too much: the dan dan noodles tasted like they'd been doused in after shave, which was too bad because the chewy, irregularly-cut noodles were really good.

But when they calibrate it right, this is some of the best spicy food in town. The best dish there for me so far is stir-fried pork belly in lots of diagonal-cut shards of leek. The belly, braised in star anise, is beautifully cooked, coming off as being as compulsively scarfable as American bacon, while the dish has a great balance of stir-fry sizzle and peppercorn tang. "Fatty beef" (the beef isn't fatty, but the broth is) with clear rice noodles came to the table submerged in peppers and looking like a mouthful of hurt, yet surprised with its subtle use of heat and the wok hay of the noodles. There's a lot of skill in this tiny place's kitchen. *What to order:* stir-fried pork belly with leek, fatty beef with clear rice noodles, mapo tofu, Chef's Special lamb ribs. **NEW**

F Fooditor's 19 Best New Places to Eat in Chinatown, 3.15.19

61. Rica Arepa

Hermosa • South American • $

4253 W. Armitage, Chicago • 773.543.3000 • ricaarepachicago.com

For years I knew arepas mainly as a sort of starchy buff pad that came on the side of a meat-centric South American meal. But the economic crisis in Venezuela has sent people from that country to Chicago, resulting in an arepa boom here that has changed my view of them as a comfy masa shell to be stuffed with tasty things, as warmly satisfying as Mexican gorditas. (Incidentally, they're gluten-free.) I've had good ones at ArePA George and Sweet Pepper, but the most charming place to have them is this utterly friendly and welcoming cafe with outside seating in good weather, which does a remarkable job of evoking the European-like plaza feel of South American cities on a cramped stretch of

Armitage. *What to order:* arepas here offer you the same half dozen ingredients (beef, chicken, cheese, etc.) in every possible combination, but the sweet spot is occupied by the signature Pabellon, with its unimprovable combo of beef, cheese, black beans and sweet plantains stuffed inside.

62. Kabab House (Iraqi Kabob House)

Albany Park • Middle Eastern • $$

4849 N. Kedzie, Chicago • 773.942.6300 • karamgrills.com

Last year I wrote about a new high-quality middle eastern restaurant called Karam Grill. It's now known as Kabab House or Iraqi Kabob House (yes, different spellings), but otherwise what I wrote last year seems unchanged:

The sign advertised "best hummus in town." I had just eaten at a place advertising "best shawarma in town," which made me check the map to see what the hell town I was actually in, so I wasn't expecting this one to be any more true. But then I saw the pita—perfectly cross-hatched from the grill. Who takes that kind of care with pita? These guys, apparently. The hummus came—and damn if they might not be right. Creamy, flavorful, it was a pleasure to scoop with my cross-hatched pita. Other dishes came— falafel, freshly fried, bright with herbs; beef shawarma was good, chicken shawarma, often dry, was even better. At the moment, they're doing the standards better than anyone else on the middle eastern strip along Kedzie. *What to order:* any standard middle eastern dish, including hummus, falafel, chicken shawarma. REVISED

63. ROOH Chicago

West Loop • Indian, Cocktails • $$

736 W. Randolph, Chicago • 312.459.7750 • roohchicago.com

The snazziest of the new higher-end Indian restaurants in Chicago occupies two brightly-colored floors of an old building right on Randolph, staking out territory for this cuisine alongside all the others in the West Loop—there's been Indian on this strip before, but it's never been as ready to compete as this place. The third U.S. restaurant for a group that has others in San Francisco and New York, there are signs of deliberate luxury in things like the truffle shavings over a pea-stuffed kulcha, but most of the menu is devoted to substance over flash, simply bringing high ingredient quality and fresh spicing to classic Indian dishes, or evolving to a next step—like the bhel puri with tuna tartare, whose combination of seafood and crunchy bits is more California than Kolkata, but works all the same. *What to order:* green pea and goat cheese kulcha, tuna bhel, gun powder scallop, cauliflower koliwada, whole sea bass. **NEW**

F The Most Famous Indian Chef No One Knows in Chicago, 10.3.19

64. Cafe Istanbul

Wicker Park, Ukrianian Village • Turkish, Middle Eastern • $$

2014 W. Division, Chicago • 773.661.9487 • mycafeistanbul.com

On my visit to Istanbul, food was earnest and fresh more than artfully clever, but one thing took those virtues to their highest point—cag kebab, the original form of Turkish döner, in which the meat, stacked sidewise, is rotated in front of a fire as the cag kebab man carefully eyes and slices off perfect crispy bits on a thin skewer. We went to Sehzade Cag Kebap in Sultanahmet twice, because who knew when we might have such a thing again?

And now here it is in Chicago—not *quite* as good as in Istanbul, perhaps, but more than good enough to be worth starting to plan a Turkish feast; the lively crowds of Turkish Chicagoans on Saturday night are a sign that you're in the right place. (Note that the same owner has a sandwich/doner shop called Istanbul Grill in Lakeview, but the menu is shorter—you want the Wicker Park location for the full spread of Turkish dishes.) *What to order:* cag "dza" kebab, doner, iskender, mujver, manti, patlican salatasi, imam bayeldi. NEW

65. Boeufhaus

West Town · Steak, Sandwiches · $$$
1012 N. Western, Chicago · 773.661.2116 · boeufhaus.com

As steakhouses grew over more grandiose downtown, this place opened to bring them back to down to earth in the city's neighborhoods, serving a brasserie-style menu as well as selling beef in its meat market up front. The steaks are very good, but the thing that wowed me the most with the care it showed was a crudité plate—between the housemade Green Goddess dressing and the gorgeous, handpicked vegetables, this was a plate that would have warmed James Beard's heart as an example of unfussy, clean-flavored midcentury American food. *What to order:* crudité, shortrib beignets. tartare of boeuf, ceci bean cavatelli, 55-day aged ribeye; at lunch, reuben, porchetta, boeuf on weck.

66. Mr. D's Shish-Kabobs

Montclare • Greek, Fast Food • $
6656 W. Diversey, Chicago • 773.637.0042

I put this fast food grill on my classics list in last year's edition, but it's gotten a new burst of publicity this year, so why not promote it to the main list—it's a rare survivor of the type of ethnic blue-collar family-run joint that used to be all over Chicago, and pass into history every year. In this place where time stopped in 1967, a whole family, from somewhere around the Mediterranean, crank out meaty sandwiches fresh from the grill, served with fresh-cut fries and a can of RC pop (do I even need to point out that they take *cash*, not Discover or Apple Pay?). My favorite is the pork kabob, four or five meaty fists of pork seasoned with Italian spices (or a bottled Italian dressing) and stuffed in a roll, but others prefer the steak sandwich, and nobody is wrong. The fries won best in the city in the Tribune recently, which won my highest honor for a listicle, which is me nodding and going, "Ehhh, they got it right this time." *What to order:* pork kabob, steak sandwich. **NEW**

67. Morena's Kitchen

Belmont Cragin • Dominican, Chickenn • $
5054 W. Armitage, Chicago • 773.622.7200

Dominican food is one of those cuisines that has existed around Chicago for a couple of decades without really being noticed that much. Morena's got a blip of fame in 2018, as much as anywhere in a far west side neighborhood is ever going to get, and the reason for that is pretty clear—it's a one-woman show where chef-owner Mirian Montes de Oca dishes up instantly likable homemade food with a room-filling smile. *What to order:* crispy fried chicken, made (when she can get it) with Dominican oregano, which dyes the juices squirting out of it a pale green; hearty stews like carne guisado and oxtail; the fish stew sancocho.

F The Fooditor Guide To The Best Eating Block in Chicago, 2018, 2.20.18

68. Minna's Restaurant

Belmont Cragin • Mexican • $
5046 W. Armitage, Chicago • 773.417.7602 • minnasrestaurant.com

Not to be confused with Morena's Kitchen a few doors west, though if the food is different the charms are much the same—a small woman-run business full of energy and good vibes. In this case it's a Mexican diner, run by what appears to be at least three generations of women in the same family, slinging homemade tortillas and plates of hearty Mexican diner food with good humor to a room full of working guys. *What to order:* chilaquiles (green or red), squash blossom quesadillas, enchiladas potosinos.

F The Fooditor Guide To The Best Eating Block in Chicago, 2018, 2.20.18

69. Pleasant House Pub

Pilsen • English, Beer, Brunch • $$
2119 S. Halsted, Chicago • 773.523.7437 • pleasanthousepub.com

A couple of years ago I wrote that one of Michelin's biggest bungles was not giving Pleasant House Bakery a Bib Gourmand designation for their incredibly satisfying, literally farm to table English savory pies, very tourist friendly, that would return change from a $10. They finally did in 2017, so now all I can say is, even Michelin recognizes how good these things are, now that you can get them with a cloth napkin and a beer in the former

Nightwood space, with beer on tap and some other items like fish & chips. *What to order:* Chicken balti pie, mushroom and kale pie, fish & chips, Welsh rarebit mac and cheese.

70. Finom Coffee

Irving Park • Coffee, Hungarian, European • $
4200 W. Irving Park, Chicago • 312.620.5010

One of Chicago's mysteries is the lack of Hungarian restaurants in the region; with the opening of this cozy coffeehouse in an historic storefront in November, their short list of hearty, paprika-spicy items now represents Hungarian Chicago, along with some items such as marrow toast that capture its spirit but cross it with artful 2018 touches (e.g., a rather liberal use of micro flowers for a coffee joint). The drink list includes novelties like a Turkish latte served with rose water and cardamom. Like Budapest before the war, this place has a lot of charm. *What to order:* lecsó (vegetable stew), marrow toast, gulyásleves (goulash), körözött.

71. Bayan Ko

Ravenswood, North Center • Cuban, Filipino • $$
1810 W. Montrose, Chicago • 773.698.6373 • bayankochicago.com

He (chef Lawrence Letrero, who worked in Sable, Untitled and other big kitchens) is Filipino; she (Raquel Quadreny) is Cuban, and this small, pretty adorable Filipino-Cuban restaurant explores both cuisines and their common ancestry in Spanish cooking, from pancit noodles liberally laced with pork to an excellent Cuban sandwich... liberally laced with pork. The smaller, appetizer-y things are almost all delectable; the Filipino dishes, perhaps a bit surprisingly, remain pretty authentic and thus not always immediately accessible, whether that's oxtail in peanuty kare-kare (with a small side of shrimp paste, if you want to dial up its funk) or luglug noodles with scallops and uni. But a blend of scarfable and challenging isn't a bad way to go. *What to order:* barbecue pork sticks, lumpia, shrimp al ajillo, lechon, Cuban sandwich, luglug noodles, flan.

F Two Heritages, Two Homelands Intertwined at Bayan Ko, 10.17.18

72. Bamyan Kabob

West Rogers Park • Central Asian, Middle Eastern • $$
5701 N. California, Chicago • 773.961.7902 • bamyan-kabob.business.site

The building on California, just off Lincoln, has been a dozen things, all pretty anonymous. So you're unprepared for the way a *caravanserai* seems to have sprouted inside it, flowing curtains and lush fake flowers and all the hospitality of Central Asia. Have a pot of tea and study the menu, which ranges from middle eastern standards (shawerma and hummus, excellent falafel) to rice pilafs and manti dumplings from Afghanistan and probably any number of other countries in the region. Whatever you choose, it will be freshly made, halal, and served with warmth that will make you want to come back whenever your travels pass through these lands. *What to order:* falafel, hummus, chicken shawerma, borscht, kabuli, pelmeni, oromo.

73. Young American

Logan Square • Filipino, Cocktails • $$
2545 N. Kedzie, Chicago • 773.687.8385 • youngamericanbar.com

Young American, located in the same block as Lula Cafe, started with CBD-infused cocktails and things like Goth bread made with blackened flour. It made for good copy for food writers, but didn't win actual diners over. The CBD cocktails are still there, but chef Nick Jirasek has reconcepted with the kind of food he was doing at Old Habits at Ludlow Liquors (owned by the same group)— Chicago blue collar comfort food, crossed with things from the Filipino half of his family. It's not only as appealing as it was at Ludlow Liquors, it's a step up in sophistication for that food (which could be a gut bomb at Ludlow)—comfy textures, interesting and contrasting flavors (including, sometimes, a surprising degree of heat). Young Americans v. 2 is a standout for bar food with some thought behind it. *What to order:* smoked clam dip, popcorn shrimp, lumpia shanghai, cacio e pepe-ish, Filipino chicken tendies. **NEW**

74. Le Sud

Roscoe Village • Wine Bar, French • $$$
2301 W. Roscoe, Chicago • 773.857.1985 • lesudchicago.com

As a resident of Roscoe Village, I was reconciled to all the really cool concepts heading straight for Logan Square. We were like a forgotten village in the countryside... so what better for our most appealing local dining choice to be than this expert neighborhood French restaurant, something you might find attached to a country inn in the provinces? Kevin McMullen, of El Ideas and The Brixton, took over the kitchen in mid-2019, but didn't miss a beat in terms of comforting flavors, good year-round but especially perfect for wintry months, while the chic interior is handsome without being needlessly trendy, and the service is unfussily grownup. *What to order:* country pate, rabbit stew with cavatelli, pan roasted duck breast, whole loup de mer, trout almondine, wood-grilled chicken. REVISED

75. Bob's Pizza

Pilsen • Pizza • $$
1659 W. 21st, Chicago • 312.600.6155 • famousbobspizza.com

Not to be confused with Robert's Pizza in Streeterville, this new place on a side street in Pilsen—*not* known as a pizza hotspot—combines a 1960s neighborhood tavern feel, black leather booths and so on, with hand-tossed thin crust pizza with a crispy bottom and a chew with heft and give. That works well with standard toppings like pepperoni or the (perhaps meant to sound funny) Grass Fed Meatball, but when I went, someone (Bob?) urged me to give the "Pickle Pizza" a try. Mortadella, housemade dill pickles, dill and cracked pepper go on a garlic cream base. It's like a deli on a pizza crust, and I loved it (though I'll admit no one else in my family was as charmed; I had a lot of it that week). It's not as wide and varied a list as Pizzeria Bebu, but give it credit for a similar fearlessness of its own. *What to order:* Bob's sausage pizza, pickle pizza, spinach pesto & stracciatella. **NEW**

76. Torchio Pasta Bar

River North, Near North Side • Italian • $$
738 N. Wells, Chicago • 312.643.0543 • torchiopastabar.com

The look of this bar-restaurant—dark and narrow and masculine enough for Frank and Dino to have hung out in —makes it look like it might have been there for a generation. In fact it's new, the invention of a (non-Italian) corporate executive and engineer who got the bug for making housemade pasta. So the comfily nostalgic setting is really there for cranking out torchio (a spiral pasta that vaguely resembles a torch), bucatini, orecchiette, radiatore and others. They have a nice chewy texture, while there's good flavor in the saucing (if, as is almost inevitable in

America, too much of it on the plate). In a neighborhood of big and grandiose places, this is the kind of hidden gem that wins you points for knowing it exists. *What to order*: "Torchio" pasta, rigatoni with plum tomato sauce, bucatini all'amatriciana, Giovanna's Bolognese. **NEW**

77. Egg-O-Holic

Noble Square, West Town • Indian, Vegetarian • $
833 W. Chicago, Chicago • 312.940.3521 • egg-o-holic.com

It's exciting that we're starting to get regionalized Indian cuisine in Chicago, and few things can be more unexpected than to find ourselves with a place devoted to the late night street/drunk food of the state of Gujarati, in a location that probably used to be a bar (now the big screen TVs show cricket). What this food turns out to be is a lot of Indian stews of various sorts, made with eggs—fried eggs, shredded scrambled eggs, sliced hardboiled eggs, accompanied by your choice of roti or American style white toast (!). I recommend going in a group, because one dish with lots of egg in it is a bit monotonous, but four people with four different things to scoop up is a bargain basement feast. The best, like the lachko (shredded green peppers and eggs and herbs) are refreshingly bright and veggie, food to start you on the road to recovery after a long night. *What to order*: lachko, egg bhurji, boil tikka, paneer gotala. **NEW**

78. The Heritage

Forest Park • American, Farm to Table • $$$
7403 Madison, Forest Park • 708.435.4937 • theheritageforestpark.com

Not to be confused with The Heritage Caviar Bar in the city, this spot on the busy restaurant and pub row of a near-in western suburb offers you farm to table dining in all its honest, earnest 2015 glory, from the white subway tiles on the wall to the familiar farmers' names on the menu. Well, I liked it then and I like it when I tried it this summer (note that chef Rick Ohlemacher has left since then, but it seems to be continuing in a similar vein). Cauliflower tempura-fried with espelette pepper, a duck egg with tuna aioli to scoop onto Publican Quality bread, a brined-almost-to-confit roasted chicken sitting on a brightly comfy salad of corn, squash and shishito peppers—this was my happy, fresh-tasting comfort food, and if it did exist in the city, it would be packed. Instead it was half full on Friday night, Forest Parkers apparently sticking more to what they know. But for city folks, this is a getaway and a change of scenery from Logan or the West Loop—you could even get there by CTA, as it's just a few blocks' walk from the end of the Blue Line. *What to order:* the dishes I liked included crispy cauliflower, corn elotes, fjord trout tartare and heritage roasted chicken, though I expect it to have evolved with both the chef change and the seasons. **NEW**

79. Heritage Restaurant & Caviar Bar

West Town • Eastern European, Seafood • $$$
2700 W. Chicago, Chicago • 773.661.9577 • heritage-chicago.com

With caviar now bring produced around the world, is it any surprise that it's now possible to have a neighborhood place that specializes in a night out with the once-precious black globules? Heritage's caviar service covers a range of price points, all accompanied by impeccable fried potato chips, sour cream and other accoutrements. Beyond the fish eggs, the all-day menu is eclectic almost to the point of randomness—pierogi made with hen of the woods mushrooms, vegetable ramen, chicharrons with cheese, in the summer a heritage tomato pie, a burger… but why complain about a place trying so hard to please? Generally things are easy to like and suit the laidback neighborhood atmosphere just fine. *What to order:* caviar, smoked sturgeon, potato pierogi, wood-grilled octopus, crispy trout.

80. Wentworth Seafood House

Chinatown • Chinese • $$
2229 S. Wentworth, Chicago • 312.808.0899 • wentworthseafoodhouse.com

With so many Sichuan restaurants in Chinatown, it's refreshing to find a new Cantonese restaurant. Wentworth Seafood House, which sounds like it could have been there forever but is only about year or two old, offers a dim sum menu and lunch specials through the afternoon, and a Cantonese menu stressing seafood at night. Salt and pepper tofu had a creamy custard-like inside under a crisp fried shell; my first bite was kind of, huh, that's pretty basic, what it says it is, and by my third bite I was in love. Yelp reviewers strongly recommended seafood pumpkin congee; I usually find congee bland but this was a chickeny broth with bits of seafood in it, and quite comforting (especially with bits of cruller to dip in it).

We dabbled around the menu, trying to taste from as many categories as we could. Xiao long bao were routine, if not frozen from a bag at least passing for same, but fried rice with dried shrimp and bits of Chinese sausage was very scarfable, and stir-fried watercress in a seafood broth with bits of preserved egg smelled like the fish section at an Asian market. I mean that in the best possible way. **NEW**

F Fooditor's 19 Best New Places to Eat in Chinatown, 3.15.19

81. Nella Pizza e Pasta

Hyde Park • Pizza, Italian • $$
1125 E. 55th, Chicago • 773.643.0603 • nellachicago.com

Slowly, Hyde Park's restaurant scene emerges from its
eternal 1986, and few things seem a cheerier sign than this
bright white Italian bar with its bulk cans of tomato sauce
for decoration and a scooter hanging over the bar. The
pizza is itself a bit of a throwback—the same authentic
Neapolitan that Nella Grassano has been making around
town since coming from Italy as the first pizzaiola at Spacca
Napoli in 2006. The crust with its chewy crunch and
speckled underside; the acidic trumpet blast of tomato
sauce; the not-too-creamy cheese and the slightly wet center
—Hyde Park doesn't need to come all the way to the
present, 2006's pizza with 60s La Dolce Vita will do just
fine for a pleasant afternoon watching soccer with an
Aperol spritzer in hand. *What to order:* Nella D.O.P., bianco
nero, prosciutto rucola, papadelle al ragu al Agnello. **NEW**

82. Ava's Italian Ice

Bucktown • Ice Cream • $
1814 W. Western, Chicago • 773.622.7200

One time I went here and had apricot Italian ice—and it
was amazing, full of subtle apricot goodness. I went back
the next week and it wasn't *quite* as good. A complaint? On
the contrary, it proves their claim to be working from
seasonal fruit—a commercial flavor base wouldn't have had
a peak one week and been a notch under that the next
week. Week after week last summer I watched for them to
be open and if they were, beelined for them across Western
Ave. traffic to see what in-season fruit they'd turned into
magical snow this week. They'll be closed for the winter,

but watch for them to return sometime in April or May. *What to order:* what's good that week.

83. Brass Heart
Uptown • Tasting Menu, Vegetarian • $$$$
4662 N. Broadway, Chicago • 773.564.9680 • brassheartrestaurant.com

Matt Kerney worked at tiny Schwa and then busy Longman & Eagle, which probably qualifies one to open a tasting menu spot in Chicago as much as anything could. Brass Heart takes over the 42 Grams space (completely remodeled) to offer an intimate tasting menu which adeptly ranges from high (wagyu and lobster) to high-low (some version of rice and beans as a signature dish). That's one side of it; the other is that it offers the city's (or maybe the world's) only vegan tasting menu, multiple courses of ingeniously constructed food which attempts to provide full flavors with the lushness of dairy and other parts of classical cooking. It's surprisingly effective, particularly in the sense of not making you aware that anything you expect is absent —a fascinating experiment for non-vegans, to see what you *have* to have to feel satisfied. *What to order:* 9 or 12 course omnivore or vegan menus, or a 6 course version on Tuesdays only. NEW

84. Red & White Wine Bar
Bucktown • Wine Bar • $$
1861 N. Milwaukee, Chicago • 773.486.4769 • redandwhitewineschicago.com

The dining room, with its concrete floor and the light of the retail wine space shining in, underpromises; the service and the food overdelivers. The staff is eager to pair your food and you with whatever interesting and unusual thing they're serving at the moment, with a particular eye toward natural wines, and you can have a very pleasant light dinner out of a few glasses and cheese, charcuterie or salads. But they can be more ambitious and succeed when they do —roasted black cod with caponata is a simple dish, as much assembly as cooking, yet it comes out beautifully prepared and entirely satisfying. *What to order:* follow your tastes and the advice of your server.

85. All Together Now

Ukrainian Village, West Town • Wine Bar, Farm to Table, Coffee • $$
2119 W. Chicago, Chicago • 773.661.1599 • alltogethernow.fun

Part wine shop, part cheese and charcuterie shop (it has ties to Madison's Underground Meats), and part hipster all-day dining spot, All Together Now is an odd duck at first glance, but a pleasant choice for when you want handmade food of high quality and veggie-forward virtue-eating. *What to order:* daytime, French Exit sandwich, smashed white bean sandwich, farro and leeks; dinner, creamed trout, molasses-glazed half chicken, chess pie tart. **NEW**

86. Taqueria El Kacheton

Belmont Cragin • Mexican • $
2446 N. Laramie, Chicago • 773.420.7892

Everyone should have a favorite little Mexican family-run spot, and this one is mine—which is to say, do I think it's greater than yours? No, but it's just fine, and I hope you'll like it and I'll like yours. The tables, with their colorful checkered cloths, are cute; the service is friendly and has just enough English; the salsa is quite hot; the handmade tortillas are warm and comfy; the chicken mole is richly chocolaty-spicy, and that's what I stick to, but I'm sure anything else they do is just fine. *What to order:* chicken mole or whatever looks good. **NEW**

F The Fooditor Guide To Mexican Food on the West Side, 6.13.17

87. Pan Artesanal

Logan Square • Bakery, Sandwiches, Mexican • $
3724 W. Fullerton, Chicago • 312.286.5265 • panartesanalbakery.com

Marisol Espinoza, the baker of the two Mexican sisters who run this cafe, went to the French Pastry School to learn classic baking technique, which is why the French-style croissants and fruit-filled danishes stand far above what you typically find in Chicago's Mexican bakeries. But don't stop there; she incorporates Mexican ingredients in baking in unique ways, like the cactus scone or the gusano bread, made with dried, ground worms—a traditional source of added protein. Add an array of sandwiches for lunch, and this is a little gem that's a nice alternative to the hipster coffee cafes of Logan Square. *What to order:* breakfast: danishes, croissants, chorizo-egg sandwich; lunch: mango ham avocado or chipotle chicken sandwich.

88. Landbirds

Bucktown • Korean, Chinese, Chicken • $
2532 N. California, Chicago • 773.697.7107 • landbirdschicago.com

The spicy-sweet glazed, frenched "lollipop" chicken wing is a Chicago thing, going back to Great Sea Restaurant on Lawrence; Eddie Lee used to eat them while helping at his father's photography studio nearby. Now he's selling his version at this no-frills, personable shop in Logan Square, going through a thousand pounds a week of hand-breaded, blanced and fried wings coating in a housemade sauce of soy, garlic and chiles. There are a few other menu choices to explore, but Lee is a man who knows one thing he wants to make well. *What to order:* wings, musubi fried rice; take the guidance on spice levels seriously. **NEW**

89. El Sabor Poblano
Rogers Park • Mexican • $
7027 N. Clark, Chicago • 773.516.4243

In Chicago, mole usually means the chocolatey Oaxacan mole negro, so the thing that's exciting about this regional Pueblan family restaurant is that it's focused on two specifically Pueblan moles—red mole poblano and especially the *pipiàn verde*, called green mole but almost mud-colored with its pumpkin seed base. The second exciting thing is the handmade tortillas, made with a yellow corn masa, and you couldn't go wrong by starting with a chicken leg in this earthy mix, accompanied by blistered fresh tortillas to scoop up extras with. There are other Pueblan specialties like tamales de ceniza, thin tamales filled with herbs (Mike Sula said epazote in his review, but the son told me hoja santa—could be either at different times), or weekends-only things like the soup guasmole, made with beef and guaje seeds. In any case, it's yours to explore, this friendly spot whose regional specificity gives it a unique place among the city's Mexican spots. *What to order:* chicken leg with pipian verde, picaditas. **NEW**

Three Wheels Noodle

90. Ora

Andersonville · Sushi, Japanese · $$
5143 N. Clark, Chicago · 773.506.2978

Neighborhood corner sushi exists all over Chicago, most of it at about the same level of unremarkable, making a steady living mainly off dressed-up rolls. Ora rises from the many places that look just like it with a higher quality and more interesting range of fish offerings than many in its price class, plus a high level of care in how it's treated. *What to order:* Come during the week for individualized counter service; on the busy weekends, you can order by dollar amount or number of pieces, and even under pressure they're pretty good at giving you a good assortment of what they have at the time. **NEW**

91. Ms. T's Southern Fried Chicken

Lakeview · Southern, Chicken, Soul Food · $
3343 N. Broadway, Chicago · 773.728.2500 · mstssouthernfriedchicken.com

Wrigleyville hardly seems like the place to go looking for soul food in this town, but the vivacious Ms. T, who used to run a Harold's franchise, cranks out impressively crispy fried chicken, fish and a few other things that go with mild sauce to satisfy your jones (it's well located for delivery on the north side). *What to order:* chicken, fish, hush puppies, corn nuggets. **NEW**

92. Three Wheels Noodle

Logan Square · Thai · $$
2339 N Milwaukee, Chicago · 773.360.8288

Before I went to Thailand I always wanted the most exotic Thai flavors—give me the tartness of tamarind, galangal, the funk of fish sauce and shrimp paste. But even on a short visit in 2018—but with the help of a food tour—I experienced a new kind of comfy dishes full of noodles and scrambled eggs, that were like Thai diner food, subtle funk but deep soul. (These were the dishes that get Americanized with too much sugar here, mostly.) Anyway, Three Wheels Noodle—the sign says Noodle and Rice—is the closest I've found to that Thai food. Add in the very hip Logan Square decor—the kitchen looks like an airplane's fuselage, the huge faces on the wall look like *Blade Runner*—and I've added a new spot to my local Thai repertoire. *What to order:* khao soi (golden curry noodle), Bring It On noodles, drunken noodles, see ewe noodle. **NEW**

93. Pisolino

Avondale · Italian, Pizza · $$
2755 W. Belmont, Chicago · 773.293.6025 · pisolinochicago.com

Chicago restaurants are so big and self-important any more that we kind of don't know what to make of a place whose modest ambitions are obvious at first glance. Pisolino is an Italian cafe, a dozen tables, pasta, pizza and panini on the menu, espresso machine on the bar, wines on the chalkboard... so what's the *angle?* There isn't one, just a couple of fresh salads, nice enough pastas, a very good fennel and orange salad, sort of Roman pizza (the crust is crispy and pretty good, the toppings are very good). It's like someone took your favorite neighborhood modern-Italian place in 1990 and beamed it unchanged into the future. *What to order:* fennel and orange salad, bucatini carbonara, orrechiete with sausage and rapini, Raquel and Donatello pizzas, butterscotch budini.

94. The Sala Pao Shop

Bucktown · Thai, Chinese · $
1909 N. Western, Chicago · 773.697.9267 · salapaoshop.com

Food halls have become one answer for a city that discourages food trucks, but I'd love to see another answer take off—stands located inside subway stations, like this one inside the vintage Art Deco Western Avenue blue line stop. Jan Purananda, whose parents had Sticky Rice, serves up fluffy bao filled with Chinese and Thai flavors, plus a daily rotation of rice bowls and some Thai iced teas. They all make a happy end to a CTA journey. *What to order:* BBQ pork bao, basil chicken bao, sticky rice mango. **NEW**

95. Spinning J Bakery and Soda Fountain

Humboldt Park · Breakfast, Bakery, Sandwiches · $$
1000 N. California, Chicago · 872.829.2793 · spinningj.com

This charming place, home to a repurposed vintage wooden bar, sweetly evokes 1920s soda fountains and lunch counters, with light sandwiches and soups and excellent pie —and real phosphates. If you have to ask what that is, just go have one right now. *What to order:* sandwiches, quiche, key lime hibiscus pie, strawberry-watermelon phosphate.

96. Panango!

Near North Side, River North · Mexican, Bakery, Sandwiches · $$
720 N. State, Chicago · panango.us

The professional branding for the casual bakery attached to Carlos Gaytan's upscale Mexican restaurant Tzuco suggests that it might turn out to be a bigger (chain) business in the end. The Mexican pastries are terrific—more like French pastries with Mexican flavors like chocolate and passionfruit. The breads—flavored with Mexican ingredients as well—are good, but pre-making the sandwiches and holding them in a cold case, like Pret à Manger, does the bread a disservice, and only one, with roast pork, really impressed me for its flavorfulness. It's early. *What to order:* all the pastries. **NEW**

97. Big Boss Spicy Fried Chicken

Bridgeport • Chicken, Sandwiches • $
2520 S. Halsted, Chicago • 312.877.5031 • bigbosschicken.com

Located on the border between Chinatown and Bridgeport, and working somewhere on the border between Chef Jassy Lee's Chinese and Central American heritages and flavor profiles, this place does very good spicy fried chicken sandwiches in a street art atmosphere, but the best play is to order them with a side of the housemade pickles—the mix of hot chicken and cooling pickles is pretty darn perfect. *What to order:* like I said, chicken sandwich with a side of pickles; also fried chicken. **NEW**

98. Astoria Cafe and Bakery

Irving Park • Eastern European, Bakery • $
2954 W. Irving Park, Chicago • 773.654.1033

Despite the New York name, this is an Eastern European family affair—a Serbian family with mom cooking in back and the cheerful daughter providing hospitality up front. What you'll mainly see on display are mom's cakes and tortes, all good and hearty in a *mittel*-European way, but the menu doesn't stop there—they also dish up crepes as well as savory things like meat-filled bureks, sarma (stuffed cabbage), the hearty soup pasulj and przenice, a kind of French toast served with feta. But if you need a true hearty breakfast (for, say, a day of coal mining), order the Komplet Lepina, which is like a Serbian version of Eggs Benedict, a hunk of bread stuffed with pork, eggs and gooey Serbian cheese… with a side of cured pork loin. It's kind of amazing —bring someone to split it with. *What to order:* Komplet Lepina, crepes, burek, pasulj, przenice.

F My Way: The Fooditor Guide To New Places on the Northwest Side, 4.17.18

99. Lola's Coney Island

Humboldt Park · Fast Food · $
2858 W. Chicago, Chicago · 773.687.9459 · lolasconeyisland.com

It doesn't seem like anyone's opening new Chicago hot dog stands these days, but at least we got a new Detroit hot dog stand. The Detroit style Coney Dog tops a pork and beef dog (unlike our all-beef ones) with convincing Detroit chili, while the Loose Burger puts the same chili on a patty. Beyond those, there's a Chicago dog, a New York dog with kraut and spicy brown mustard, and even a Maine lobster roll on Fridays, plus some real ringers for a cement-floored stand like this, like a chopped salad and avgolemeno soup. And of course there's Faygo pop on the side. *What to order:* start with the Detroit favorites. **NEW**

Tandoor at ROOH Chicago

RESTAURANTS BY TYPE

ASIAN
10. S.K.Y.
15. Proxi

BAKERY
5. Fat Rice
19. Middle Brow Bungalow
45. Cellar Door Provisions
87. Pan Artesanal
95. Spinning J Bakery and Soda Fountain
96. Panango!
98. Astoria Cafe and Bakery

BARBECUE
26. Honey 1 BBQ
59. Flat & Point

BEER
19. Middle Brow Bungalow
35. Band of Bohemia
42. Kimski
69. Pleasant House Pub

BREAKFAST
24. Xoco
46. Lula Cafe
48. 5 Loaves Eatery
95. Spinning J Bakery and Soda Fountain

BRUNCH
5. Fat Rice
10. S.K.Y.
11. Virtue

14. Daisies
24. The Bristol
35. Band of Bohemia
40. Big Jones
41. Funkenhausen
46. Lula Cafe
56. Cebu
69. Pleasant House Pub

CENTRAL ASIAN
72. Bamyan Kabob

CHICKEN
48. 5 Loaves Eatery
67. Morena's Kitchen
88. Landbirds
91. Ms. T's Southern Fried Chicken
97. Big Boss Spicy Fried Chicken

CHINESE
5. Fat Rice
44. La Mom Kitchen
60. Szechwan JMC
80. Wentworth Seafood House
88. Landlords
94. The Sala Pao Shop

COCKTAILS
8. Kumiko
15. Proxi
34. Bar Sótano
63. ROOH Chicago
73. Young American

COFFEE
45. Cellar Door Provisions
50. Hai Sous Vietnamese Kitchen/Cà Phê Dá
70. Finom Coffee

CUBAN
71. Bayan Ko

DOMINICAN
67. Morena's Kitchen

EASTERN EUROPEAN
42. Kimski
79. The Heritage Restaurant & Caviar Bar
98. Astoria Cafe and Bakery

ENGLISH
69. Pleasant House Pub

EUROPEAN
28. Table, Donkey and Stick
70. Finom Coffee

FARM TO TABLE
6. Smyth & The Loyalist
14. Daisies
17. Elizabeth
24. The Bristol
45. Cellar Door Provisions
46. Lula Cafe
78. The Heritage
85. All Together Now

SANDWICHES
24. Xoco
36. Tempesta Market
50. Hai Sous Vietnamese Kitchen/Cà Phê Dá
87. Pan Artesanal
95. Spinning J Bakery and Soda Fountain
96. Panango!
97. Big Boss Spicy Fried Chicken

SEAFOOD
20. mfk.
79. The Heritage Restaurant & Caviar Bar

SOUL FOOD
11. Virtue
48. 5 Loaves Eatery
91. Ms. T's Southern Fried Chicken

SOUTH AMERICAN
25. El Che Steakhouse & Bar
61. Rica Arepa

SOUTHERN
11. Virtue
40. Big Jones
41. Funkenhausen
91. Ms. T's Southern Fried Chicken

SPANISH
20. mfk.
30. Bar Biscay
49. Income Tax

STEAK
25. El Che Steakhouse & Bar
65. Boeufhaus

SUSHI
4. Kyōten
43. Mako
90. Ora

TASTING MENU
1. Schwa
2. Jeong
3. Oriole
6. Smyth & The Loyalist
7. Elske
8. Kumiko
9. Wherewithall
12. Blackbird
17. Elizabeth
23. Entente
83. Brass Heart

THAI
47. Aroy Thai
55. Sticky Rice Northern Thai Cuisine
92. Three Wheels Noodle
94. The Sala Pao Shop

TURKISH
64. Cafe Istanbul

VEGETARIAN
39. Politan Row
83. Brass Heart

VIETNAMESE
50. Hai Sous Vietnamese Kitchen/Cà Phê Dá
57. Nha Hang Viet Nam

WINE BAR
20. mfk.
22. Munno Pizzeria & Bistro
28. Table, Donkey and Stick
30. Bar Biscay
49. Income Tax
74. Le Sud
84. Red & White Wine Bar
85. All Together Now

RESTAURANTS BY LOCATION

DOWNTOWN

NEAR NORTH SIDE
37. Pizzeria Bebu
53. Mozzarella Store
54. The Albert
76. Torchio Pasta Bar
96. Panango!

RIVER NORTH
23. Entente
24. Xoco
34. Bar Sótano
76. Torchio Pasta Bar
96. Panango!

STREETERVILLE
54. The Albert

WEST LOOP
3. Oriole
6. Smyth & The Loyalist
7. Elske
8. Kumiko
12. Blackbird
13. Monteverde
15. Proxi
25. El Che Steakhouse & Bar
39. Politan Row
43. Mako
51. Gaijin
52. Bellemore
63. ROOH Chicago

NORTH SIDE

ALBANY PARK
62. Kabab House

ANDERSONVILLE
33. Passerotto
40. Big Jones
90. Ora

AVONDALE
9. Wherewithall
45. Cellar Door Provisions
93. Pisolino

BELMONT-CRAGIN
67. Morena's Kitchen
68. Minna's Restaurant
86. Taqueria El Kacheton

BUCKTOWN
24. The Bristol
38. Tortello
82. Ava's Italian Ice
84. Red & White Wine Bar
88. Landbirds
94. The Sala Pao Shop

EDGEWATER
49. Income Tax

HERMOSA
61. Rica Arepa

HUMBOLDT PARK
95. Spinning J Bakery and Soda Fountain
99. Lola's Coney Island

IRVING PARK
70. Finom Coffee
98. Astoria Cafe and Bakery

LAKEVIEW
20. mfk.
91. Ms. T's Southern Fried Chicken

LINCOLN PARK
18. Galit
21. Boka

LINCOLN SQUARE
17. Elizabeth
35. Band of Bohemia
47. Aroy Thai

LOGAN SQUARE
4. Kyōten
5. Fat Rice
14. Daisies
19. Middle Brow Bungalow
27. Osteria Langhe
28. Table, Donkey and Stick
31. Pretty Cool Ice Cream
45. Cellar Door Provisions
46. Lula Cafe
58. Mi Tocaya Antojeria

Tortello

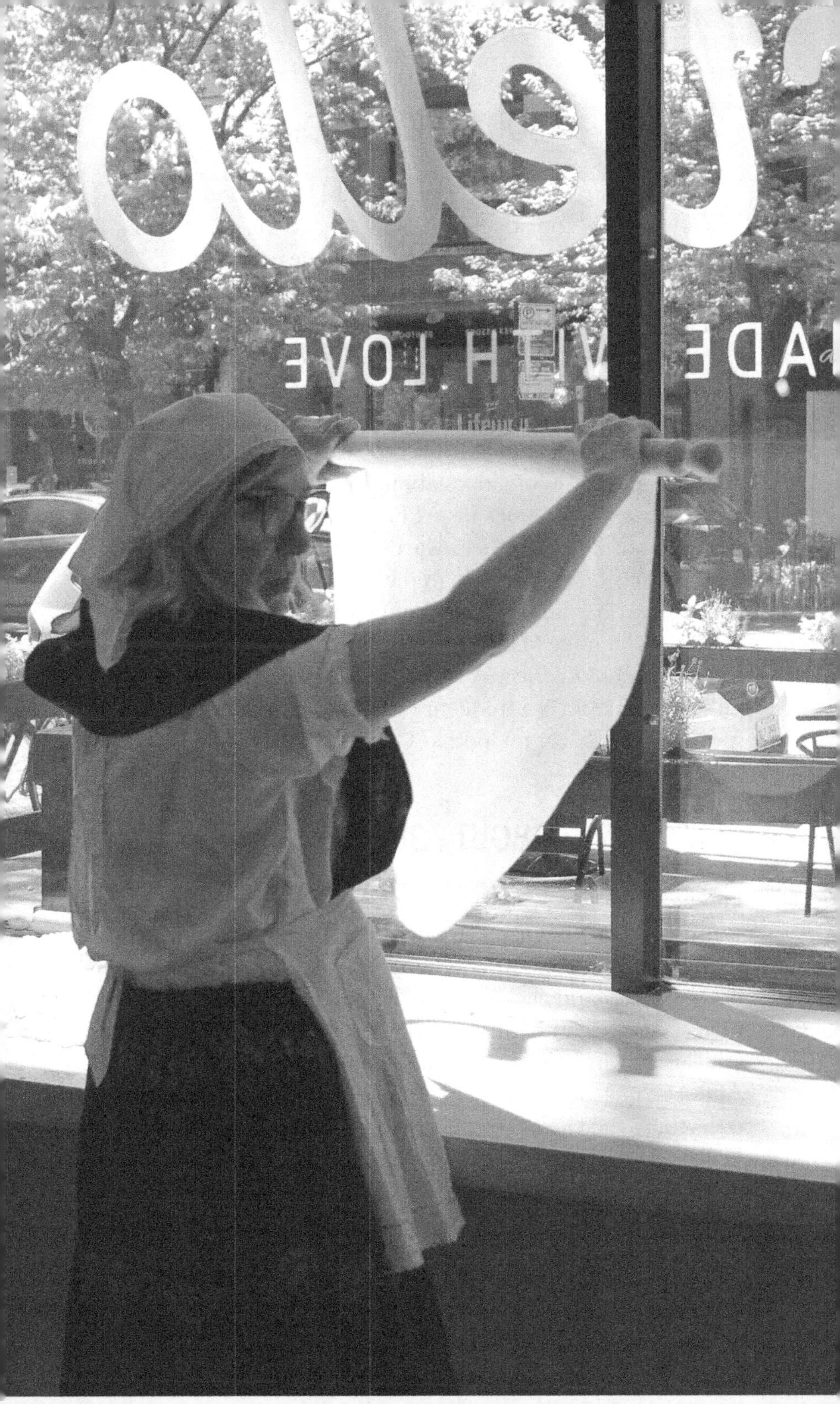

ABOUT THE AUTHOR

Michael Gebert is the editor and publisher of Fooditor. He was a writer for top ad agencies in Chicago for many years, and began writing about food online in the early 2000s, becoming one of the founders of the online chat site LTHForum and writing for publications such as the Chicago *Reader* and *Time Out Chicago*. He was the Chicago editor of New York magazine's Grub Street, and had a regular column on food for the *Reader*.

His blog and series of videos about food subjects, *Sky Full of Bacon*, earned two James Beard Foundation Award nominations, among other awards; as the videographer for the Chicago *Reader's* Key Ingredient chef challenge video series, he won a James Beard Foundation Award in 2011. He has written for *Chicago* magazine, *Saveur, Maxim, First We Feast, New Food Economy*, Air Canada's *En Route* and other publications, and is a frequent radio/podcast guest and speaker/moderator on food in Chicago.

ABOUT FOODITOR

Fooditor is Chicago's locally grown, Peter Lisagor-Award-winning online magazine about one of the most exciting food scenes in the country. Going beyond the usual food news, listicles and clickbait, Fooditor digs into Chicago's food scene with in-depth interviews, analysis, stories about Chicago's celebrated and up-and-coming chefs, and more. And it roams all over the city to introduce Chicagoans to everything the city's food culture has to offer. Follow Fooditor on Twitter (@fooditor), Facebook and Instagram (@fooditorchi).